the American Dimension

Cultural Myths and Social Realities
2nd Edition

W. Arens, SUNY, Stony Brook
Susan P. Montague, Northern Illinois University

ALFRED PUBLISHING CO., INC.
15335 Morrison Street
Sherman Oaks, CA 91403

"Rituals at McDonald's" used with permission from
Natural History, January, 1978. Copyright the American
Museum of Natural History, 1978.

"Gender Differences in Graffiti: A Semiotic Perspective"
used with permission of Pergamon Press Ltd. Reprinted
from *Women's Studies International Quarterly*, Vol. 3,
No. 2/3, 1980, pp. 239–252.

Alfred Publishing Co., Inc.
15335 Morrison Street
Sherman Oaks, California 91403

Current printing last digit: 10 9 8 7 6 5 4 3 2 1

Library of Congress Cataloging in Publication Data

Main entry under title:

The American dimension.

    1. United States—Popular culture—Addresses,
essays, lectures. 2. United States—Civilization
I. Arens, W., 1940–   II. Montague, Susan P.
1942–
E169.12.A42   973.92   80-26335
ISBN 0-88284-119-X

Contents

PREFACE

The student of anthropology rightly expects that his course of study will introduce him to the variety of human experiences. Yet rarely does this include the study of American culture. This is an unfortunate oversight, because American culture is as rich and as deep as any other. Consequently, we feel that this collection of essays, by native Americans, fills a gap in a discipline that purports to examine the cultural universe. The analyses offered will not only tell us something about our hidden selves, but will help us to understand others in a more meaningful way.

The following essays are concerned primarily with the message content of mass media, which present a body of highly stabilized information aimed at a large, voluntarily participating audience (i.e., television and film viewers). Thus it can be assumed that what is presented reflects the ideas and interests of a large number of Americans. Further, the information is readily accessible, far easier to obtain than data collected by interviewing many individuals.

These essays treat one particular body of mass media data, the information transmitted through entertainment channels, which includes television programs, motion pictures, magazines, and staged performances such as plays and sports events. Entertainment productions deal with the content of interpersonal relationships, that is, how individual actors respond to others in various situations. Even impersonal topics such as politics and economics are treated in terms of the actions of specific individuals, and how their decisions affect their lives as well as those in their immediate social circle.

The entertainment media are frequently accused of being shallow and void of meaningful context, but this is pseudointellectual pretension. In fact, entertainment deals with the most important issues Americans face: how to best live their daily lives, what it means to be an American and to live in American society.

These issues underlie more commonly recognized social issues such as what type of political or economic system is most appropriate for our society. It is not too surprising that although we disapprove of political censorship in societies that directly equate morality with the existing political order, we at the same time heavily censor our own entertainment media. Television is the most obvious case, with pretaping and bleeps to avoid inadvertent intrusions of objectionable material. Movies are also censored and coded for various audiences. Magazine publishers face at least threats of prosecution when their subject matter, usually sex, is perceived as a threat to social mores. Rock stars are arrested with considerable frequency, and concertgoers may be hassled by the police. Questions of major changes in sports, such as the advisibility of allowing women and men to compete with each other, or the use of drugs to enhance performance, are treated in terms of their implications for the morality of the entire society.

In short, the mass media constitute a forum for depicting and, to a certain extent, debating current morality. They offer the viewer situational models that can be adapted and used in the individual's own life. Far from being shallow or meaningless, popular entertainment examines what it is to be human in our society, dissecting and reconstructing the most basic social situations and providing an ongoing discussion of our very essence. The media provide a gold mine of useful information for the analysis of American culture.

A few of the essays move outside the mass media to consider information contexts wherein the populace takes an active role. The health food movement, the phenomenon of McDonald's restaurants, and the practice of writing graffiti in toilets all fall into this category. But the topic remains the same: the content of interpersonal relationships. These essays explain some of the ways in which the kinds of messages transmitted in the mass media are utilized by Americans to build action scenarios in their own lives.

We hope that the essays will be insightful and will raise significant questions for further analysis. Because the essays deal with our own culture, the reader is also the native, and therefore has the opportunity to consider and debate the analysis and conclusions arrived at. We offer the book as a beginning effort in what we think will be a fruitful exploration into the topic that has always interested us the most: ourselves.

We would be remiss in our responsibilities as editors not to conclude this preface by acknowledging our debt to the many individuals who have assisted us. The majority of essays were originally presented at the 1974 meetings of the American Anthropological Association at the symposium, "North of the Border." We were privileged to have with us as discussants Professor Robert Manners of Brandeis University and Professor Harold W. Scheffler of Yale University. Their comments and reflections on the papers were appreciated by all concerned and have been incorporated into this presentation. They deserve our collective thanks and appreciation for sharing their thoughts with us. We hope that we have succeeded in putting their advice into practice by examining the seemingly trivial side of American social life without being trivial ourselves.

We were fortunate in having the expert assistance of Jeffrey Steinberg and the services of Mari Walker for an unending supply of bad puns and good typing. Finally, we would like to dedicate this book to our respective mentors. Although they have not participated in this project directly, they provided us with the intellectual perspective that resulted in the study of American cultures.

INTRODUCTION

When Ralph Linton described anthropology as a "mirror for man" he pinpointed one of the field's most distinctive features, its reflectivity. Anthropology is reflective because it allows us to look at people, removed from us by time or by space, in order to better see ourselves. The others may be foreigners living in far off lands, man's fossil ancestors, and even his closest nonhuman relatives, the primates. Thus anthropologists work to obtain a vision of our humanity by looking in the mirror of distant relatives. This is why the field is reflective.

But if anthropologists look at others, what is to be made of a book wherein American anthropologists look directly at their own, American, way of being human? Such a book does make sense in that the goal of anthropological inquiry is ultimately self-knowledge. Successful cultural anthropology should yield insights into the anthropologist's own culture.

Anthropology began as the study of human evolution. The field's first task was the construction of a picture of man's primitive past. This involved gathering together diverse bits of evidence from many sources. From the outset anthropologists assumed that the evidence lay outside the immediate world of modern Western man, since he was thought to represent the most highly evolved stage of human development. Some anthropologists sought evidence about man's physical evolution, and some about his social and cultural evolution. To social/cultural scholars two sources seemed to promise to yield useful evidence. One was archaeology, the excavation and examination of the remains of past societies. The other was the study of exotic, or primitive, peoples. These were presumed to possess simple social and cultural organizations and were thought to be living examples of earlier stages in modern (Western) man's sociocultural development.

Today anthropologists know that the living "primitives" are really nothing of the kind. All peoples, no matter how small their group size or simple their technology, live in rich, complex, sophisticated sociocultural milieus. Thus the initial investigation was found to be somewhat misguided. Despite this discouraging discovery, social and cultural anthropologists did not discard the idea of studying exotic peoples in order to obtain self-knowledge. Instead, the reflective study of foreigners was turned to a newer series of specific tasks. Prominent among them is that of learning exactly what culture is and how it works. This task is grounded in a somewhat different view of the nature of reflectivity than was the original evolutionary task. The early evolutionists studied foreigners and foreign lifeways *rather than* themselves and their own lifeways, because they thought that the evidence for man's past lay outside their own highly evolved world. Modern anthropologists, who realize that all living peoples possess fully evolved social and cultural forms, look to foreigners to see things that they might miss by looking only at themselves. Thus the modern "mirror for man" is a two-way mirror which anthropologists use to see themselves and others in order to gradually build a picture of human nature.

The need for cultural anthropologists to examine directly their own cultural world is now clearly recognized. Francis L. K. Hsu, recent president of the American Anthropological Association, goes so far as to grant it priority. He says:

> I firmly believe that systematic study of the ethnographer's own culture is the first order of business in his or her training. It should be required of every graduate student working for the Ph.D. in anthropology, or it can be made the first intensive field experience. (1979:526)

Hsu takes this position because he is concerned about ethnocentrism, which is the tendency for people to assume that their own culture is intellectually and morally superior to all others. Ethnocentrism acts like a set of blinders to slow, even prevent, the ethnographer from seeing foreign cultural worlds accurately. Sometimes people are aware of their own ethnocentric biases, but more often ethnocentrism functions in an unconscious manner. The aspects of their own sociocultural order that they take for granted are those aspects that people are most apt to be ethnocentric about. Hsu thus suggests that anthropologists can help themselves to learn foreign ways by first making a conscious effort to learn the content of their own cultural systems.

This book, then, grows out of both ends of the modern anthropological reflective process. The anthropologists whose essays it contains have all worked in foreign cultures, and bring insights gained from that work to an examination of American culture. At the same time, they are trying to consciously see aspects of American culture that they have not seen previously so that when they return to work again among foreigners they will more clearly see the foreign worlds they investigate.

The anthropological investigation of American culture does pose some problems. How should it be done? What aspects should be chosen for study? Let's take these issues one at a time.

The traditional methods of data collection in social and cultural anthropology are geared to work done in small communities located in societies with limited populations. The mechanics consist of fieldwork and participant observation. Participant observation means not only watching and talking with the people, but also joining in their activities insofar as it is possible. Since the community and society are relatively small, and since residence is usually for an extended period of time, hopefully the anthropologist can provide a thickly detailed in-depth report about the interests, activities, and lifeways of the people studied. The stumbling block to applying these tools to the study of Western society is the immense size of the population. Anthropologists are still able to live among the natives and do intensive work with a few of them, but how can it be known whether the findings have general applicability?

One solution is to make no claims about general applicability. Some scholars, like W. Lloyd Warner, went ahead and applied traditional field methods to the study of American communities, and then suggested that scholars looking at other American communities might find it useful to look for the things they found. This proved to be a fruitful approach. Warner's picture of the class structure of Yankee City had a great deal of impact on American social science, and many scholars explored his findings in the context of other American communities. Still, many anthropologists felt uneasy about the applicability issue. They recognized that sociologists had found a solution in the use of social statistics. These data consist of information produced through questioning a representative sample of a larger population. Insofar as the sample is truly representative, the information is generalizable to the larger population itself. However, the statistical approach does not yield the in-depth data that anthropologists prefer to work with. The gathering of information suitable to statistical analysis requires standardized questioning procedures, which virtually precludes the kind of take-it-where-the-informant-will-go interviewing that brings anthropologists their rich results.

Fortunately, in recent years there have been some new solutions offered to the problem of the general applicability of data collected from a small group of informants. The tremendous developments made in communication theory have proved applicable to the analysis of cultural systems. Every communication system turns around a core of basic units and rules for combining them. This core must be known to all who use the system if communication is to occur. Otherwise it would be like two people trying to play a game together with one of them using the units and rules of checkers and the other using the units and rules of chess. Cultures are communication systems, and anthropologists can at least hypothesize that, like other communication systems, cultures too turn on a basic core of units and rules known to all the users. Thus anthropologists working to ascertain the nature and content of this core do not have to worry overly about the representativeness of their sample.

In addition, communication systems are generative. This means that, as with checkers and chess, the relatively small number of units and rules that form their cores can be manipulated to yield a large number of action scenarios. Anthropologists "mapping" the culture of a large population society can use the variation they see around them to describe the generative process. Thus even the diversity found in American lifeways can be turned to good analytical use.

But exactly what aspects of American culture should anthropologists study? Fieldworkers have long found rituals to be fruitful sources of cultural information. The term ritual is defined in various ways by various anthropologists, but most would agree that rituals are standardized performances, and that they transmit basic moral messages. The Catholic ritual of the mass, for example, is a standardized performance that conveys important Christian ideas about man's relationship to God. Not all rituals, however, occur in a sacred, or religious, context. Americans use many secular performance vehicles to deliver moral messages. Included are such prosaic vehicles as football and baseball games, television soap operas and situation comedies, along with political inaugurations and college graduations. Even such seemingly mundane and utilitarian events as buying hamburgers at McDonald's can be analyzed as secular rituals, since they too constitute standardized performances with moral overtones. All these and a host of others combine to make up the moral texture of the world in which we live.

Fortunately, the American anthropologist is in a strong position to study the rituals in his own culture. While he must guard against taking things for granted, he has his experience with foreign rituals to help him see sharply. In addition, he tends to have greater exposure to American rituals than to foreign rituals. The maximal field stay in a foreign locale is usually two years. This means that the field worker must try to analyze rituals that, at best, he has seen only a few times, and at worst he has not seen at all, but only been told about. Further, he knows more about the contexts of American rituals. While rituals deliver basic messages, they nonetheless often presuppose a good deal of information on the part of both participants and viewers. Mass, for example, presupposes knowledge about the Judeo-Christian principles of sin and salvation. A non-Westerner unfamiliar with these ideas might find it confusing.

This book, then, constitutes an attempt by American anthropologists to extend our comprehension of American culture, and in so doing to extend our knowledge of all culture. The authors ask things like: Why is McDonald's America's leading fast food chain? Why is baseball one of the two quintessential American sports? Why are so many Americans interested in health foods? Why do so many Americans find soap operas fascinating? By seeking answers to these questions and countless others like them American anthropologists work to build the reflective picture that will ultimately tell us what it means to be cultural, or human, beings.

*W. Arens has done fieldwork in Africa, and has published on ethnicity and change in various "learned" journals. As Bill Arens, he watches a lot of football on television. The following essay is an attempt to alleviate the guilt this has caused. The primary question is to determine the meaning and effect of the cultural messages which are transmitted from the TV screen to the dormant bodies exposed to the images. An abbreviated version of this essay also appeared in the sports pages of the **New York Times**. As a result, subsequent letters to the paper raised serious allegations about the author's patriotism, intelligence, and masculinity.*

PROFESSIONAL FOOTBALL

An American Symbol and Ritual

W. ARENS

O, you sir, you! Come you hither, sir. Who am I, sir?
OSWALD. My lady's father.
LEAR. 'My lady's father'! my lord's knave! you whoreson dog! you slave! you cur!
OSWALD. I am none of these, my lord; I beseech your pardon.
LEAR. Do you bandy looks with me, you rascal? [striking him.]
OSWALD. I'll not be strucken, my lord.
KENT. Nor trip'd neither, you base football player.

King Lear, Act I, Scene 4

A school without football is in danger of deteriorating into a medieval study hall.

—Vince Lombardi

Attitudes toward football players have obviously changed since Shakespeare's time. Today the once "base football player" occupies the throne and rules the land. In fact, to have played too many games without a helmet seems to be a prerequisite for high office in our country. The prominent role football assumes in our society deserves comment. I would contend that although only a game, it has much to say about who and what we are as a people.

Although I am a professional anthropologist by training and have carried out fieldwork in another culture, this essay owes its impetus to the years I have sat in front of a television watching hundreds of football contests. Out of a feeling of guilt, I began to muse in a more academic fashion about this game and turned to the numerous books written by players and also to the rare anthropological accounts of sport in other societies. This has led me to believe that if an anthropologist from another planet visited here he would be struck by the American fixation on this game and would report on it with the glee and romantic intoxication anthropologists normally reserve for the exotic rituals of a newly discovered tribe. This assertion is based on the theory that certain significant symbols are the key to understanding a culture. It might be a dreadful thought, but nonetheless true, that if we understood the meaning of football we might better understand ourselves.

I emphasize a symbolic analysis because this game that intrigues us so much is engaged in by relatively few, but highly skilled individuals. Most of us at one time or another have played golf, tennis, basketball, softball, or even baseball, but only the "pros" play football. Touch football must be discounted because it lacks the essential ingredients of violent physical contact and complexity of game plan. The pleasure derived from football therefore is almost totally vicarious. This sport's images and messages satisfy our collective mind, not our individual bodies.

An appreciation of this argument requires an initial short detour in time to examine the evolution of this American sport from its European origins. The enshrined mythology states that the game was first played by a group of English soldiers who celebrated their victory over a Viking settlement by entering the losers' burial ground and using the skulls of the enemies' dead in a kicking match. Sometime later, an animal's inflated bladder was substituted for the skull, and the sport of "Dane's Head" became known as football. During the early Middle Ages, the game was a disorganized all-day competition between neighboring towns. The ball was placed midway between two villages and the object was to kick it along the countryside into the village and finally onto the green of the opposing community for a score. The game became so popular with the English peasantry that Henry II banned the pastime in the twelfth century because it interfered with the practice of archery. The sport was not reinstated until the seventeenth century, by which time the longbow had become an obsolete weapon.

According to Reisman and Denny (1969), who have charted the game's evolution, the kicking aspect remained dominant until 1823 when, as popular legend has it, a scoundrel named William Ellis, of Rugby School, "with a fine disregard for the rules of football, as played in his time, first took the ball in his arms and ran with it." This innovation on soccer was institutionalized at the school, and shortly thereafter was adopted by others; hence the name "rugby"—and the association of this sport in England with the educated elite.

Although both games were exported to America, only rugby was modified in the new setting. The claim has been made by the participants, and officially adopted by the National College Athletic Association, that the first intercollegiate game took place between Rutgers and

Princeton in 1869. However, since that contest followed soccer rules, the honor of having played the first game of what was to emerge as American football rightly should go to Harvard and McGill in 1874, when rugby regulations were the order of the day. In the remaining decades of the nineteenth century, the sport began to take on a more American form as a definite line of scrimmage and the center snap replaced the swaying "scrum" and "heal out" of English rugby. This meant that possession of the ball was now given to one team at a time. However, the introduction of the forward pass in the early years of this century signaled the most radical break with the past. These revisions on rugby resulted in greater structure and order, but at the same time more variety and flexibility, because running, kicking, and forward passing were incorporated as offensive maneuvers. Football had become an American game.

As a result of this process, football has emerged as an item of our cultural inventory that we share with no other country but Canada, where it is not nearly so popular. Does football's uniqueness and popularity say something essential about our culture? Rather than dismiss this question as trivial, we should be aware that we share our language, kinship system, religions, political and economic institutions, and a variety of other traits with many nations, but not our premier spectator sport. This is important when we consider that other societies have taken up baseball, a variation of cricket, and basketball, a homegrown product. Like English beer, the American brand of football is unexportable, even to the colonies. No one else can imagine what the natives see in it. On the other hand, soccer, the world's number one sport, has not been a popular success in America. In a peculiar social inversion, though, the educated and well-traveled American middle class has taken some interest in this sport of the European working classes. Nonetheless, football is uniquely American and little else can be included in this category.

Also, football, as compared to our language and many values, is not forced upon us. It is an optional aspect of our culture's inventions, which individuals choose to accept. Our society, like any other complex one, is divided by race, ethnicity, income, political affiliation, and regionalism. However, 79 percent of all the households in the country tuned in the first Super Bowl on TV, implying that the event cut through many of the divisive factors just mentioned. Personally, I can think of precious little else that I have in common with our former or current president, with a rural Texan, or an urban black other than a mutual passion for this game. Football represents not only "Middle America," as is so often claimed, but the whole of America. When we consider football, we are focusing on one of the few things we share with no one outside our borders, but do share with almost everyone within it.

The salient features of the game and of the society that created and nourishes it reflect some striking similarities. The sport combines the qualities of group coordination through a complex division of labor and minute specialization more than any other that comes to mind. Every sport exhibits these characteristics to an extent, but in football the process has surely reached the zenith. Every professional and major college team finds it necessary today to include a player whose only function is place kicking, and another for punting. Some have individuals whose sole responsibility is to center or hold the ball for the point after touchdown. Football is also a game in which success now demands an extensive reliance on sophisticated electronic technology from telephones to computers while the match is in progress. In short, football, as opposed to its ancestor, rugby, epitomizes the spirit and form of contemporary American society.

Violence is another of our society's most apparent features. This quality of American life and its expression in football clearly accounts for some of the game's appeal. That football involves legitimate bodily contact and territorial incursion defines it as an aggressive sport par excellence. It is hardly surprising therefore that books by participants are replete with symbolic references to war. For example, Jerry Kramer, a Green Bay Packer during their glory years of the 1960s, divides his book, *Instant Replay*, into the following sections: Preliminary Skirmishes; Basic Training; Mock Warfare; Armed Combat; War's End. Frank Leahy, a former coach of Notre Dame and in his time a living symbol of America, wrote in his memoirs:

> . . . the Stars and Stripes have never taken second place on any battlefield. With this in mind, we ask you to think back and ask yourself where our young men developed the qualities that go to make up a good fighting man. . . . These traits are something that cannot be found in textbooks nor can they be learned in the lecture room. It is on the athletic fields that our boys acquire these winning ways that are as much a part of the American life as are freedom of speech and of the press (1949: 230).

Mike Holovak (1967), a former coach of the New England Patriots, waxed even more lyrical in reminiscing about his World War II military service. He refers to those years as the time he was on "the first team" in the "South Pacific playground" where the tracers arched out "like a long touchdown pass" and the artillery fired "orange blobs—just like a football."

To single out violence as the sole or even primary reason for the game's popularity is a tempting oversimplification. There are more violent sports available to us, such as boxing, which allows for an even greater display of legitimate blood spilling. Yet, boxing's popularity has waned over the last few decades. Its decline corresponds with the increased interest in professional football, in which aggression is acted out in a more tactical and sophisticated context. Football's violence is expressed within the framework of teamwork, specialization, mechanization, and variation, and this combination accounts for its appeal. A football contest more adequately symbolizes the way in which our society carries out violence than does a sport that relies on naked individual force. An explanation of football's popularity on the basis of violence alone also overlooks the fact that we are not unique in this respect. There have been many other violent nations, but they did not enshrine football as a national symbol.

Although the "national pastime" may not have suffered the same fate as boxing, interest in baseball has also ebbed. If my analysis of football is correct, then baseball is not in step with the times either. The action in baseball does not entail the degree of complexity, coordination, and specialization that now captures our fancy. I think this is what people mean when they say that baseball is boring. The recent introduction of the designated hitter and the occasional base-running specialist who never bats or fields are moves to inject specialization and heighten the game's appeal to modern America. In essence, baseball belongs to another era, when life was a bit less complicated.

To return to our original interest, one final point must be made on the symbolism of football. Earlier I wrote that football represented the whole of America and overcame traditional differences in our society. However, the importance of the division between the sexes, which has more recently become part of our consciousness, was not mentioned. Football plays a part in representing this dichotomy in our society because it is a male preserve that manifests and symbolizes both the physical and cultural values of masculinity. Entrance into the arena of football competition depends on muscle power and speed possessed by very few males and beyond that of most females. Women can and have excelled in a variety of other sports, but football generally excludes them from participation. It was reported in a local newspaper that during a game between female teams the players' husbands appeared on the sidelines in women's clothes and wigs. The message was clear: if the women were going to act as men, then the men were going to transform themselves into women. These "rituals of rebellion" involving an inversion of sex roles have often been recorded by anthropologists. It is not surprising that this symbolic rebellion in our culture was aimed at a bastion of male supremacy.

If this argument seems farfetched, consider the extent to which the equipment accents the male physique. The donning of the required items results in an enlarged head and shoulders and a narrowed waist, with the lower torso poured into skin-tight trousers accented only by a metal cod-piece. The result is not an expression, but an exaggeration of maleness. Dressed in this manner, the players engage in handholding, hugging, and bottom patting, which would be ludicrous and disapproved in any other context. Yet, this is accepted on the gridiron without a second thought. Admittedly, there are good reasons for wearing the gear, but does that mean we must dismiss the symbolic significance of the visual impression? The game could just as easily be played without the major items, such as the helmet, shoulder pads, and cleats. They are as much offensive as defensive in function. Indeed, in comparison rugby players seem to manage quite well in the flimsiest of uniforms.

The preceding discussion puts us in a better position to ask the question hinted at earlier—are we in effect dealing with an American ritual of some meaning? The answer depends upon how ritual is defined. A broad anthropological view suggests that it is a standardized, repetitive activity carried out for the purpose of expressing and communicating basic cultural ideals and symbols. A ritual therefore does not necessarily imply communication with the supernatural. The inauguration of a president or the playing of the national anthem are common examples of nonreligious rituals in America. An objective evaluation of the problem also demands recognizing that an act can have a sacred and a secular character at the same time. Consequently, at one level, football can be viewed simply as a sport and at another level as a public ritual. Considering some of the players' activities from this perspective furnishes some interesting and supportive observations.

If we view the game as a ritual and therefore in some respects as a sacred activity, we would expect the participants to disengage themselves from the profane world of everyday affairs. This is a common aspect of ritual behavior in any part of the world. Especially relevant for the participants is the avoidance of what anthropologists refer to as "pollution"—an impure ritual state—as the result of contact with contaminating acts or situations. Association with this profane realm renders a participant symbolically unfit to engage in a sacred performance.

In many rituals performed entirely for and by males, sexual contact with females must be avoided. Abstinence under these conditions is almost a cultural universal because the sexual act is an expression of man's animal or profane nature. In many a rite of passage for boys about to enter adulthood, the participants are taken out of the community, isolated from the opposite sex, and may not be seen by them. In other societies, prior to a significant activity such as the hunt or warfare, the community members are admonished to refrain from sexual behavior for fear of disastrous consequences. Is it really surprising then that in the world of sport, and with football in particular, sex before the event is viewed with suspicion? In this context I am reminded of Hoebel's (1960) statement that: "The Cheyenne feeling about male sexuality is that it is something to be husbanded and kept in reserve as a source of strength for the great crises of war." This compares well with the attitude at the virtually monastic world of football training camps. At these facilities all of the players, including those married, are sequestered together during practice days. They are allowed to visit their wives, who must be living off the grounds, on Saturday night only, since there is no practice on Sunday. As is to be expected they must return to the all-male atmosphere on Sunday evening in consideration of Monday's activities. The result is that sex and football, the profane and the sacred, are segregated in time and space. During the season a variation of the procedure prevails. The players and staff spend Saturday night together since the contest takes place on Sunday. In each instance there is a clear-cut attempt to avoid the symbolic danger of contact with females prior to the event.

This was impressed on me when I traveled with my university's team by chartered bus to a game to be played at the opponent's field. Since there were a few unoccupied seats, two of the players asked the coach if their girlfriends could ride along. He said in all seriousness that they could not ride to the game with us, but that they could join us on the bus on the way home. A writer who spent the season with the Rice University football squad mentioned a similar instance (Tippette, 1973). When the team bus pulled up in front of the dormitory where they would spend the night on the opponent's campus, a number of the girls from the college entered the vehicle and began to flirt with the players. The Rice coach, who was in an accompanying car, stormed onto the bus and ordered the girls off immediately. He then told the players that they should have known better, since the incident was a dirty trick instigated by their foe. Dirty trick or not, somebody planned the exercise, well aware of the unsettling effect that it would have on the team.

One further example is from the professional arena. Describing the night before the first Super Bowl, when the Green Bay Packers were allowed to bring along their wives as a reward for championship play, Jerry Kramer wrote: "My wife's been here for the past few days, and so has Chandler's. Tonight we're putting the girls in one room, and Danny and I are sharing one. It's better for the girls to be away from us tonight. We're always grumpy and grouchy before a game" (1968).

There are, of course, some perfectly reasonable arguments for segregating the players prior to a game. For one, the coaches argue that they are assured that the team members get an undistracted night's sleep. Thus it is assumed that the players will be better able to concentrate on the upcoming event. At the same time, when these vignettes are considered, the theme of possible pollution through contact with females is not altogether absent. In any event, the inhibition of sexual activity prior to an athletic event has no apparent scientific rationale. The latest position based on research argues that sex is actually beneficial, since it induces a more restful night's sleep.

The New York Times recently reported that a British physician who has advised and interviewed his country's Olympic competitors mentioned that one informant admitted setting the world record in a middle distance track event an hour after sexual intercourse. Another confessed that he ran the mile in less than four minutes an hour and a half after the same activity. One must look beyond rationality for an explanation of the negative attitude toward sex on the part of the elders who control professional football. However, if we grant that the sport involves a significant ritual element, then the idea does make some sense. From this standpoint scientific reasoning is not relevant.

Accounts of rituals in other cultures also indicate the prevalent belief in symbolic contamination through contact with illness or physical imperfection. Examples of this sort of avoidance also crop up in football. Players report that those who become sick to their stomachs in the summer heat of training camp are avoided and become the objects of ridicule. In a similar vein, participants are rightfully admonished to stay away from an injured player so that the trainer can attend to him. However, they do not appear to need the advice since after a momentary glance they studiously avoid a downed colleague. Injured, inactive players on the team I was associated with as faculty sponsor were not allowed to mingle with the active participants during the game. The loquacious professional Jerry Kramer also writes that when he was hurt and disabled, he felt like an "outsider," "isolated" and "separated" from the rest of the group. Others have written that they were ignored during these times by their teammates and coaches. I do not want to push this argument too far because there are many sound reasons to explain this patterned reaction. At the same time, I can think of similar arguments for the behavior of people in other cultures after having come into contact with illness or death.

Eating is another profane act, since it is a further indication of our animal nature. As in every society, contact with certain foods renders an individual unfit to participate in rituals. However, in contrast to sexuality and physical imperfection, nourishment cannot be avoided for any length of time. Instead, under controlled conditions, the act of eating is incorporated into the ritual, and the food becomes charged with a sacred character. Consequently, not just any type of food is acceptable, but only specified types with symbolic significance may be ingested by ritual participants. What would be more appropriate in our society than males eating beef prior to the great event? Imagine the scorn that would be heaped upon a team if it were known that they prepared themselves for the competition by eating chicken.

The problem with a purely functional interpretation is that this meat, which, it is believed, must be eaten on the day of the competition, is not converted into potential energy until hours after the game has ended. Although the players must appear for this meal because it is part of the ritual, actually very few eat what is presented to them. Instead, in contradiction to the ritual experts, the participants prefer a high-energy snack, such as a pill, which they realize has more immediate value. Nevertheless, those who control the players' behavior, as in the other instances, adhere to a less functional course by forcing their charges to confront a meaningful symbolic substance. If this situation were presented to an anthropologist in the heart of the Amazon, I wonder how long it would take to suggest ritual cannibalism on the part of the natives.

I have tried to make it clear that I am well aware that there are a number of secular, functional explanations for the behavior that has been described. However, it bears repeating that a ritual has a variety of levels, components and consequences. The slaughter of a white bull during a rite of passage for males among cattle-keeping people in Africa has an obvious nutritional benefit for those who consume it. At the same time, though, this does not obviate the ritual significance of the act. If I am making too much of the symbolic element of American football, then perhaps we ought to reconsider the ease with which we accept this type of analysis for other supposedly simpler cultures. Accounts of team log racing among the Shavante Indians of Brazil as an attempt to restore harmony to a social order beset by political divisions (Maybury-Lewis, 1967) and the analysis of cock fighting in Bali (Geertz, 1972) as an expression of national character, have caused little stir. Unless we consider ourselves something special, our own society is equally suited to such anthropological studies. It is reasonable that if other people express their basic cultural themes in symbolic rituals, then we are likely to do the same.

References
Geertz, Clifford, 1972, "Deep Play: Notes on a Balinese Cockfight." *Daedalus.* Winter.
Hoebel, E. Adamson, 1960, *The Cheyenne.* New York: Holt, Rinehart and Winston.
Holovak, Mike, 1967, *Violence Every Sunday.* New York: Coward-McCann.
Kramer, Jerry, 1968, *Instant Replay.* New York and Cleveland: World Publishing Company.
Leahy, Frank, 1949, *Notre Dame Football.* New York: Prentice-Hall.
Maybury-Lewis, David, 1967, *Akwe-shavante Society.* Oxford: Clarendon Press.
Reisman, David and Denny, Reuel, 1969, "Football in America: A Study in Cultural Diffusion." In J. W. Lory, Jr. and G. S. Kenyon, eds., *Sport, Culture and Society.* New York: Macmillan.
Tippette, Giles, 1973, *Saturday's Children. New York: Macmillan*

I had been looking at images of personal success in juvenile pulp fiction and in sports, particularly football. I was interested in success models in rock music, but knew little about them. Robert knew a great deal about rock music and rock musicians, and offered to help me. The paper's outline emerged as it became apparent in our conversations that the success models attached to football and rock were, to a large degree, the inverse of one another.

FOOTBALL GAMES AND ROCK CONCERTS

The Ritual Enactment of American Success Models

SUSAN P. MONTAGUE
and
ROBERT MORAIS

This paper stems from a particularly insightful comment made by anthropologist Clifford Geertz about ritual. He writes that rituals are "not only models *of* what . . . [men] . . . believe, but also models for the believing of it. In these plastic dramas men attain their faith as they portray it" (1966: 29). Anthropologists have long recognized that myth and ritual function as vehicles to remind people of the basic ideology that underlies society's organization. Geertz touches on the still remaining question of faith: How is it that people become convinced that the ideology presented to them is actually truthful and correct? This question has remained unexplored, largely due to the anthropological conception of "primitives" as people who live in an ideologically monolithic universe. It is assumed that in the absence of alternative ideologies the question of faith does not arise. But this conceptualization is too naive, and certainly cannot handle questions of how faith in the existing social system is generated in societies (such as our own) that offer a variety of alternative ideologies.

Geertz does not elaborate on his idea, but his comment provides a starting point for exploring the question of why Americans find such disparate performances as football games and rock concerts so emotionally compelling. Unfortunately, informants cannot provide an adequate explanation to account for their attraction to these phenomena. This has left scholars with the task of coming up with indirect explanations, which most often are psychological, and focus on the American predilection toward violence. Various writers differ on just why Americans find violence so stimulating and desirable, but they agree that this factor does attract Americans. However, these explanations are inadequate because they fail to account for why certain standardized expressions of violence are so much more popular than others.

More importantly, the explanations miss the point. Football games and rock concerts are standardized cultural performances. Viewers find them compelling insofar as they embody significant messages. From this perspective, it is striking that the symbolic content of both these entertainment forms is heavily oriented toward the definition of success in our society. In this paper, we argue that it is impossible to directly verify in everyday life that the tenets of American success models are correct. Actors cannot readily prove to themselves that application of the models will in fact result in success. Consequently, faith in these models must be generated in some other way. This is done through symbolic validation, which is embodied in, among other things, ritual performances including football games and rock concerts. We will examine how these performance modes provide validation of American success models.

To begin it is necessary to examine the concept of success. Success is an articulating concept bridging the gap between, on the one hand, the American cosmological model of the social universe and, on the other, actor-grounded behavioral models. The cosmological model, based on traditional Christian theology, portrays a perfect universe created by God, functioning according to His laws. Man, however, violated these laws out of greed; therefore, he must wage a never-ceasing battle against his human failing. Due to his flawed character, he can never achieve God's perfection, but the price of relaxed vigilance is personal and social disaster. This model underwent gradual modification, which culminated in the late nineteenth century in the scientific-physicalist revolution wherein the laws of nature competed with and partially replaced the laws of God. However, the scientific-physicalist model of the cosmos compounded man's difficult situation, since the laws of God manifest two useful properties missing in the laws of nature. First, they are directly revealed and written down in wholly legitimized sacred books. Second, they are moral laws, which provide direct guidelines for man's behavior. The laws of nature are neither directly revealed nor moral, but instead must be discovered through an indirect process of experimentation. Further, since they are physical and not moral laws, men must also find a means for deriving behavioral guidelines from them.

The more pertinent problem for the individual is to translate universal behavioral guidelines, however formulated, into specific actions. In contemporary American culture, the concept of success constitutes one bridge between these two levels, facilitating the conversion of the general into the specific and vice versa. It does this in two ways, first by stating criteria by which the two levels are to be articulated, and second by defining a social feedback system that provides the actor with a means for monitoring the adequacy or inadequacy of his behavior. The feedback system demands our attention first.

Until the late Middle Ages, this mediation between the individual and the universal was the monopoly of Catholicism's monolithic institutional structure, and was expressed through the concepts of grace and salvation. The mediating ability was embodied in anointed individuals who participated in rituals of direct spiritual communion with God. This relationship also legitimized their role as moral arbiters of people's behavior. However, with the rise of Protestantism, the mediating role of the priest was greatly diminished, and in theory each individual was left to confront God directly and alone. This in fact meant that behavioral monitoring gradually moved outside any one given institution and was taken over by society at large. However, the result, which is still with us, is a nebulous feedback system that is both impersonal and indirect. If there is no oracle to consult, there can be no one person the actor can turn to for authoritative interpretation. Instead, feedback is provided by an intricate system of social rewards, anonymously conferred. The actor himself must attempt to monitor his behavior by examining how well he is doing in the process. This means that there must be a reward currency, and indeed there is—the so-called status symbol.

Because the reward system is indirect and impersonal, it is difficult for any given actor to verify that it actually works. According to the ideology, the system functions automatically. But how can the individual be assured that he is actually receiving his just and due reward? Further, while the rewards are conceived of as coming from society at large, they are actually conferred by a number of independent institutions. This raises the problem of standardization, since again it is difficult for the actor to determine whether or not he would receive the same reward if he worked for a different institution. Thus, in order for the system to be accepted by society's members as suitable and just, two directly unverifiable points must somehow be verified: first, that it works, and second, that it works uniformly across the board.

The other feature of the success concept is that it functions to bridge the ideological gap between universal law and the individual's behavioral guidelines in such as way as to facilitate the construction of behavioral rules that are consonant with cosmological law. This is accomplished by avoiding the question of the actual content of the universal law, and focusing instead on the motivation that underlies that content. The motivation is love. Just as the universe was created out of God's love, so the individual who acts with love can assume that he is behaving properly. Ironically, this device, which is appropriate to the Christian model of the universe, is even more important for the formulation of behavioral guidelines under the scientific-physicalist model, which does not actually contain any motivational component. Since scientific-physicalist laws are not social laws, it is difficult to derive behavioral interpretations directly from them. This difficulty enhances the value of a cultural mechanism that avoids the direct confrontation of universal law and individual behavior. Thus our culture fosters and reinforces the nature-love equation, even though that equation is not necessarily valid.

The concept of success shifts the problem of formulating behavioral guidelines from correct interpretation of universal law to correct application of universal motivation. This means that the actor and society must define which behaviors are loving. This type of definition constitutes the subject matter of success models.[1] Let us look at how the two success models embodied in football and rock define loving behavior.

Within the traditional American success model, love is defined as altruistic self-sacrifice. The properly oriented actor dedicates his life to working to improve the lives of others. In its more general form, this means that men hold jobs in the world of commerce, and women run the house and raise children. Success is defined in terms of men's work accomplishments. Women do not participate directly in the success system, but measure their status in terms of that of their husbands' accomplishments. The success system rewards moral character, which is manifested for men through work, and for women by domestic performance. A proper marriage is one that matches the moral character of the partners. Given such a union, the reward to the man can validly extend to cover the woman.

This model not only defines proper behavior, but also improper. A popular "success" author informs us that: "In time I came to recognize four basic causes for failure among salesmen; they apply equally, of course, to the pursuit of success in any line of endeavor. They are: illicit sex, alcohol, deception, and stealing" (Stone, 1962:133). Other writers on contemporary morality and success go further, and condemn smoking and gambling. Such acts are seen as indulgences that deter the individual from the path of altruistic self-sacrifice, and thus lead to failure.

The second success model, which we call the creative model, is the converse of the first. It argues that love is manifested through self-expression, rather than altruistic self-denial. Each individual possesses unique talents, and by allowing these to flower, he makes his contribution to the world. In this system, creativity replaces altruism as the valued personal commodity. This model is directly in line with scientific-physicalism, and its earliest manifestations in American pulp literature convert the ideal worker from the dedicated drudge (Alger's bank clerks and busboys) to the explorer, inventor, and scientist (Stratemeyer's Tom Swift and Don Sturdy): actors bent on discovery of the laws of the physical world. The traditional model is a straightforward application of the Protestant Ethic, and the creative model is a response to the adoption of scientific-physicalism.

The creative model raises the same sort of difficulties that plague scientific-physicalism itself. If natural laws are difficult to discover and verify, it is also difficult to specify how to socialize individuals capable of discovering and verifying them. The valued, but routine, tasks under the traditional model can be accomplished by virtually anyone who works at them hard enough. However, creativity is more than a matter of hard work. It involves personal inventiveness, based on a recombination of elements drawn from the actor's past experiences that gives him insight into a hitherto unsolved problem. It is impossible to predict precisely which elements the creative actor will draw together to obtain his fruitful insight, which means that any and all personal experiences are appropriate, whether or not society has previously defined them as moral or immoral. Further, creativity is not amenable to a rigid timetable, and it is difficult to argue that the actor should do any specific thing at any given time. Both these facts are socially unpalatable. As a result, although the creative model appeared in America in the early twentieth century, it was not until the late 1960s that its logic was pushed to completion with the argument that the truly moral member of society is the one who orients his behavior toward "doing his own thing."

With this background, let us look at how the success models are presented and validated in football games and rock concerts. In another essay in this collection, Arens has examined football as ritual, and we shall draw on some of the points he makes. He notes that football is a uniquely American game, but more than that, a cultural feature that distinguishes us from other peoples with whom we share a good many cultural traits, including language. In the United States, football is an extraordinarily popular phenomenon. Arens suggests that this is because football reflects characteristics that have a high priority in American culture: technological complexity, coordination, and native informants stress as a captivating feature of football, is not unique to the sport. What is unique is that the violence is "expressed within the framework of teamwork, specialization, mechanization, and variation." In short, to push Arens's observations a bit further, the football team looks very much like a small-scale model of the American corporation: compartmentalized, highly sophisticated in the coordinated application of a differentiated, specialized technology, turning out a winning product in a competitive market. Football ideology bears out this analogy. Successful football coaches frequently function during the off-season as business-management consultants. Some, such as Phil Krueger, a coach at USC, preach that the value of football lies not in the game itself, but in its effectiveness as a vehicle that prepares men for successful business careers (Fiske, 1975:66). Indeed, the late Vince Lombardi, coach of the perennial champion Green Bay Packers, spent a good portion of his off-season delivering inspirational lectures to middle-management on how to be a winner and rise to the top.

If there is good reason to conclude that Americans watching football are watching a model of their own work world, the question that confronts us is why Americans should actually choose to spend leisure time in this pursuit. The function of leisure as we ordinarily think of it is to get away from work. We argue that at least two factors account for this seemingly peculiar phenomenon. First, football, as a small-scale enactment of the commercial structure and process, renders visible and directly comprehensible a system that is far too large and complex to be directly comprehended by any individual. Even economists, specialists who devote themselves to attempting to obtain an overview of the structure and processes of the American economy, find the task impossible. The ordinary individual is of course at a loss as to how to begin. It is likely that he finds it difficult even to comprehend the internal structure of the company that employs him. This difficulty is a concomitant of the size and complexity of corporations in contemporary America. Football, through a reduction of scale and visual presentation, solves these dilemmas through concrete expression. The viewer, following the progress of teams within a league, can comprehend the functioning of the entire system. In addition he can watch a single team, his team, and observe its organization and performance as an internally coherent entity. Insofar as football is directly equated with the business world, the invisible and incomprehensible is rendered visible and comprehensible. It is inferred by the viewers that the processes that are seen to work in one system also operate in the other.

The second reason Americans spend leisure time watching their symbolic work world is an extension of the first. If the structure and processes that govern the world of football are equated with those of the world of commerce, then the principles that govern the actor's success on the football field must also apply in the world of work. As indicated above, Krueger feels that football is invaluable precisely because it trains men for success in business. But, as Fiske notes, the players are objects of respect and admiration, and "the values which they represent are emulated by their male peers" (1975:65). The audience, too, learns by watching the players. "Peers" in this instance include a widely heterogeneous population of American men. As Arens comments, "Personally, I can think of precious little else that I have in common with our former or current president, with a rural Texan, or an urban black other than a mutual passion for this game. Football represents not only 'Middle America,' . . . but the whole of America." The values that are held up to this widely diversified audience are strikingly similar to the values of the traditional success model. The greatest football coaches are not to be seen with talent significantly superior to that on other teams. Rather, fine coaches inspire their men on to greater heights of dedication, hard work, and self-sacrifice. The televised game commentary (often provided by former idols) and the press reports focus largely on the teams' training. As Arens points out, it is here that football becomes extremely ritualistic, in the sense that the elements selected for positive comment actually have little to do directly with improving the athletic skills of the players. Instead, they are elements symbolic of dedication, hard work, and most of all, self-sacrifice for the good of the team. Let us see how this works.

Football players are required to report to summer training camps each year to prepare for the fall playing season. The purpose of the camp is to improve player skills, develop team coordination, and get the players into condition to undergo the rigors of game combat. While team coordination is probably the most significant rational activity, both the camp schedule and the publicity place equal, if not greater, emphasis on the development of physical toughness. "Hitting," or physical collision with an adversary, is an emphasized activity. At the same time, while it is clear that hitting is an important component of the game, players express fears of suffering injuries that might sideline them during the playing season or end their careers. However, they remain, despite the validity of their fears, under heavy pressure to hit during training. Refusal to do so is taken as a sign of cowardice, lack of dedication, refusal to be self-sacrificing for the team. Actual signs of physical incapacity are intrepreted in the same manner. Players shun their injured comrades, and one insider reports that his college coach accused him of cowardice for refusing to compete after sustaining a broken neck. The epitome of the truly great player, held up for others to emulate, is Joe Namath, who supposedly quarterbacked the underdog Jets to a Super Bowl victory when he was sleeping in the living room of his parents' house because his knees were so bad he could not climb the stairs to his second-floor bedroom. His personal pain did not deter him from accomplishing the almost impossible on behalf of his team.

In addition, great emphasis is placed on forms of self-denial. During the training period players are prohibited from indulging not only in illicit sex, but also licit sex, by being segregated from their wives. Also, the players must not smoke or drink. A movie version of training camp shows team members sneaking out after bed check for a few beers at a local tavern like naughty boys on an adventurous escapade. Gambling is also taboo at all times. The football commissioner went so far as to threaten to ban Joe Namath from competition until he sold his interest in a New York bar and restaurant, which numbered among its clientele several suspected syndicate gamblers.

All of these self-sacrificing, self-denying behaviors are utilized as indices of player and team worthiness. The audience is told repeatedly that winning teams deserve to win, and do win, because their players are dedicated, hard-working, and self-sacrificing. These attributes are stressed even though the true problem of the game lies in the effective application of a complex division of labor. While this is recognized in football commentary, it is not stressed to the extent that the attributes of the success model are. Players often complain that the public, which eats up their self-sacrifices, is not as interested in the content of the various different highly skilled roles required to play the game. This makes sense because the viewer can directly comprehend specialization: he too works at a specialized job. What he cannot comprehend as easily, but what is of greater personal interest, is how the traditional success model actually works. The discrepancy here is between the problem of the game, coordination, and the problem of the viewer's life, behavioral guidelines. Football's popularity rests to a large part on the demonstration of the components of the success model at work, rather than on the concrete realities of the game itself.

Football validates the success model by staging a real event in which the principles of success are shown to work as promised by society. The contest actually happens before the viewer's eyes. The reality of the event is then transferred to the ideology of the success model, which is presented as accounting for the winning team's superior performance. Of course, there is a sleight of hand going on here, because "the best team always wins." The team that wins is not necessarily best; it is best because it wins. In order to set the stage for the legitimacy of the assertion that the best team does indeed win, the teams must rigidly and publicly adhere to behaviors symbolic of the success model during their training. It can then be argued that a team's superior performance is consonant with the expectations of the success model. The burden of proof switches to the losers: If the team that abided by the rules wins, then the team that loses must have failed to dedicate itself seriously enough.

Football not only provides the viewer with a working demonstration of the traditional success model, but also of the accompanying monitor-reward system. Again, the actor who cannot directly comprehend the structure of the business world, or even that of his own company, where he must compete for success, cannot directly verify that this system works. This explains why a good deal of football commentary is devoted to a careful statistical monitoring of each player's performance. Players' accomplishments are compared and contrasted with those of fellow team members and competitors. Rewards in the form of salary and recognition are then extended as a result of this evaluation. Again, insofar as the equation is drawn between football and business, the viewer is reassured that the system really works, for he sees actors being dispassionately and accurately monitored and rewarded according to the merits of their performance. He can also appreciate that the monitor-reward system is standardized and thus equitable.

Rock as a performance mode shares many of the basic characteristics of football. Although rock is not a uniquely American phenomenon (it has been enthusiastically received in other countries), it began here. The book *Rock Dreams* portrays the five kings of rock on its cover. Two are Americans: Elvis Presley and Bob Dylan. The other three are English: John Lennon, Mick Jagger, and David Bowie. Contemporary rock may be dominated by the English, but it grew from roots in American blues, and has, even in the hands of foreigners, retained its preoccupation with American culture. Rock, like football, thus is essentially an American phenomenon.

The recording industry is one of America's largest businesses, and its profits are anchored solidly in rock music. The avid buyers and listeners are just as inarticulate about their fascination with rock as are football fans about their sport. The release of power is also a common feature, although in rock it is accomplished through complex coordinated sounds rather than by physical violence. Armed with instruments, voices, and microphones, the Rolling Stones become the power equivalent of the Pittsburgh Steelers.

Although it is more difficult to sharply differentiate rock from other types of music than football from other sports, this is consonant with the creative success model. Rock bands face the problem of putting out a product that is qualitatively, not quantitatively, unique. There is only so much room for originality within the framework of straight rock. Performers solve this problem by amalgamating elements from other musical modes into their presentations. However, the wholly impregnable kings are the purists: Elvis, Lennon and Jagger. Significantly, artistic success within the rock world can be measured by getting one's picture on the cover of *Rolling Stone,* the rock newspaper, named after the purest of the pure.

Just as football preaches the traditional success model, rock preaches its opposite, the creative success model. An analysis of the ideology of rock as presented by the five superstars illustrates this point. The idols epitomize creativity derived from self-indulgence. The rock press focuses on how the stars satiate themselves, in contrast to the football press, which focuses on how players deny themselves. *Shooting Stars,* a book of rock star portraits, shows no one practicing or rehearsing. The entire book contains only ten or eleven pictures of stars performing or recording. The rest of the pictures are devoted to leisure activities: sleeping, lounging, drinking, traveling, partying, and picnicking. Performer interviews also generally fail to consider the work that goes into actually producing rock music. The image of the rock band is that of a collection of individually talented players who simply get it together musically. The frequent dissolution of rock groups is presented as an inevitable concomitant of the difficulties inherent in the continued association of individually creative people, each bent on "doing his own thing."

Self-indulgence is expressed through overt participation in activities that are taboo under the traditional success model. Performers both drink and smoke, often onstage, and make no secret of drug use. The most significant departure from the self-denial tenets of the traditional success model is in the area of sex. Football players are restricted from sexual activity during training and before a game. The converse is true for rock stars. The asexual rock star is a contradiction in terms because sexuality is the idiom of power in rock music. The star is expected to behave in an overtly sexual manner, suggestive onstage and promiscuous offstage. While the congratulatory crowd may go so far as to carry their favorite football players off the field after a dramatic victory, rock stars are physically attacked by hordes of would-be lovers, each bent on securing some token of intimate physical contact—a kiss if possible, a piece of hair or clothing, if not. The freshly scrubbed, girl next door cheerleader, whose formal role is to rally the team on to victory during the game, is replaced in the rock world by the whore-like groupie, whose formal role is to sleep with the star after the performance. Groupies have no place in the performance itself, because the star onstage is expected to direct his sexuality toward the audience. Elvis led the way in the 1950s with his pelvic contortions, but his gyrations were mild compared to Jagger and Bowie, the current kings. There is a telling scene in the movie *Gimme Shelter,* of Jagger watching the warm-up band, Ike and Tina Turner, on the backstage video monitor. He becomes annoyed when Tina begins to powerfully pantomime oral sex with her microphone. To the star, a warm-up band should build up the audience, not bring it to a climax.

Though rock lyrics also treat other topics, they are often blatantly sexual. To a fan any Stones song is great, but "Satisfaction," "Let's Spend the Night Together," "Brown Sugar," and "Honky Tonk Woman" are the real classics. Similarly, Dylan's most frequently played "oldie" on AM radio is "Lay Lady Lay." "Suffragette City," a song about a man being interrupted by a friend during intercourse, is one of Bowie's most popular audience numbers.

Obviously, the validation problem facing rock is different from that facing football. The traditional success model is fully consonant with the tenets of the success concept. However, the monitor-reward system is not really geared to handling creativity. Creativity is not amenable to precise statistical measurement, since it is a qualitative phenomenon. It can be measured only on some scale of social importance, but even this presents problems, because any given creation may or may not have much relevance at the time of its inception. The actor's contribution may thus go unheralded for years, perhaps forever. Further, the monitor-reward system is wholly ungeared to monitoring and rewarding the self-indulgence held to be a prerequisite of the creative act. These difficulties cast a doubt on the merits of the creative success model, for it would seem less consonant with the concept of success than the traditional model. However, the dual-component feature of the success concept supplies a way out. Remember that the concept contains both the monitor-reward system and the behavior motivation component. Rock argues that the traditional success model may be consonant with the monitor-reward system, but that it is not, and by definition cannot be, consonant with the behavior motivation

component, love. This is because the traditional success model is competitive.[2] For every football team that wins, another goes down to
defeat. Rock makes explicit this fact that in the real world the few win,
the many lose—hence the prevalence of wars, famine, poverty, and
social injustice. In the rock world, competition, a virtue under the
traditional success model, is transformed into the scourge of mankind,
the essence of evil. This means that those who achieve "success" by
adhering to the tenets of the traditional model are not really successful.
Theirs is a hollow accomplishment. Further, traditionally successful
individuals who tout their own virtues are either hypocrites or naive
fools. Jagger presents the devil as a far more sympathetic character
than the powerful people who would shun him while piously espousing
traditional goodness; unlike them, the devil is straightforward about
the damage he does. The unhypocritical idealist is, according to Bowie,
the person who would "Kill for the Good of the Fight for the Right to
be Right." He would not only slaughter his enemies who, fools themselves, are only fighting for the same thing, but also make unnecessary
grief for those who love him: "she kneels before the grave. A brave
son—who gave his live to save the slogan."

Rock lyrics not only point up the negative consequences of competition for mankind, but also for the competing individual himself.
The most the traditionally successful actor can hope for is retaliation.
As Jagger puts it, "Under my thumb, the girl who once had me down."
If he commands admiration, he also inspires jealousy. Bowie writes of
band members eyeing their guitarist-lead singer, Ziggy Stardust: "And
so we bitched about his fans, and should we crush his sweet hands."
More commonly, the person who achieves success is portrayed as
living a hollow, lonely life, isolated from love because he has devoted
himself to excelling over his fellows, rather than helping them. Probably the most powerful indictment is contained in Dylan's "Ballad of a
Thin Man," in which a conscientious, hard-working, successful man
winds up totally lost and disoriented in the hostile environment of his
own making, and is sneeringly taunted with the fact that he knows
something is happening but he doesn't know what it is. Hell has rarely
been more powerfully portrayed in any medium.

Rock begins validating the creative success model by discrediting
the traditional model as not really loving. However, this is only the
stage setting for the more important validation, a dramatic demonstration that the creative model does itself meet the love criterion. This
demonstration is of a different sort from that found in football, where
the audience watches the model being acted out by the two teams in
competition. In contrast, with a rock concert the audience itself participates in the drama. Performers address the audience, and with its
responses it becomes part of the performance. The rock star attempts
to wed himself and the audience into an experience of love. Instead of
merely seeing others and generalizing from them to himself, the audi-

ence member is encouraged to join with others and experience with them.

Loneliness, caused by isolation from others, is defined in the world of rock as the essence of nonlove, and it is by breaking down the barrier of isolation that the performer creates the emotional experience of love. The audience expects this breakdown and takes steps to initiate it even before the performer comes onstage. People talk with those sitting near them, and often smoke the same "joint," which is passed among total strangers. The first task of the performer, then, is to establish some sort of personal bond with the audience. A typical example is Jagger coming onstage after several warmup bands. He apologizes for the long delay, and explains that he has been chafing to get onstage, just as the audience has been yearning for him to appear. Rock performers not only allude to feelings that they and the audience share, they also talk in language heavy with the symbolism of interpersonal bonds. Audience members are not strangers, they are brothers and sisters, friends, fellow dope smokers.

The order of material in the concert is aimed at gradually heightening the performer-audience bond. Bowie, noted for his masterful stage performances, begins with songs of alienation and gradually intersperses sexual songs, building toward the salvation climax, "Rock and Roll Suicide." This song in turn encapsulates all that has gone before, beginning with a portrayal of the anguishing loneliness of everyday existence, and winding up with the ringing affirmation: "You're *not* alone, gimme your hand! And you're *wonderful,* gimme your hand!" On a typical night, throngs surge forward, their hands outstretched, and as he takes them, one after another, each audience member can share in belonging, being valued, being loved. The audience leaves the warm, intimate satisfaction of the theater to confront the cold, competitive, lonely world outside, yet is reassured that love can be realized, for it has just happened.

The rock audience, like the football crowd, is asked to generalize from one set of experiences to another, from the professional performance to his own life. However, the two generalizations differ radically. The football fan is encouraged first to equate two separate systems, and then how individuals function within them. The key relationship is between the individual and the system. Rock, though, does not ask the audience to equate systems since it is ideologically antisystem. Instead, the rock fan is encouraged to equate one actor, the star, with another, himself. The key relationship is individual to individual. On the contrary, the football fan can watch the contest without ever identifying with any given player. However, there is no rock without the star, no fan without his personal favorite performer or performers. Indeed, as opposed to a football contest, the rock concert lacks a broader organizational context because it stands apart from the system. The concert is simply an event without meaning beyond the "happening," whereas a football game has meaning for the future actions of a whole host of teams in the larger context of league competition. The lack of context that characterizes rock concerts is itself an important part of the message encouraging individuals to relate to one another. Rock implies that context should always be subordinated to people. The rock performer takes a collection of individuals who have no particular reason beyond their common humanity for wanting to relate to one another, and tries to turn them into a community of love. It matters little that the community is highly transitory. The argument is that all people are the same but unable to perceive this fact, because so much of their time is spent participating in various competing systems. The star, freed from systemic context, demonstrates both that love can be realized, and how to go about experiencing it. The members of the audience need only keep their sights set firmly on this goal and emulate the rock star, and they too will be able to create and enjoy love as he does, which is the essence of true success.

In this paper we have outlined the content of two mutually contradictory success models. While we have not traced the historical development of each in detail, we have noted that the creative model has gradually developed as an increasingly complete inversion of the traditional model. However, the complete development of the creative model has not caused the traditional model to become outmoded or to fall into disuse. The question then is, why does our society possess and utilize two contradictory success models? We argue that this is the case because neither strikes a workable mean between the individual's and society's needs, and that they err in opposite directions.

The traditional model (which ironically is associated with a personalized, Christian, model of the universe) sacrifices the individual and his emotional satisfaction to society. The creative model (associated with an impersonalized, scientific-physicalist model of the universe) sacrifices society for the sake of the individual. These points are illustrated with reference to rock and football, which expect the performers to adhere rigidly to only one of the two models.

The problem with the traditional model is the degree to which the individual is expected to deny himself pleasure and emotional fulfillment and still lead a personally rewarding life. Football exposes point out that far from building character, the game produces sadomasochistic brutes. Players are transformed into so many hunks of moving meat to be exploited and then discarded when their selfsacrifice has rendered them physically useless. No consideration is given to their needs as people (i.e., to their feelings). They become human machines that are expected to tolerate and mete out punishment. Participants turned writers argue that football players face a choice: to reject the ideology of the game, or to reject their own humanity. The most common solution is a compromise. When players appear in public they adhere to the game's ideology, and in private

consciously violate it by indulging in the taboo behaviors often characteristic of the creative success model.

In contrast, the weakness of the creative model is the extent to
which it encourages each individual to "do his own thing," rather than
perform routine, but socially necessary, tasks. Any society can contain
only so much freedom and anarchy. Rock performers find themselves
in a double bind. Ironically, while they publicly epitomize the creative
success model, their work demands that they succumb to the tenets of
the traditional success model. They must practice regularly, make frequent public appearances, show up for concerts and play the same
songs over and over again. In general, they have to subordinate their
individual or even collective desires to those of their manager, recording company, and ever-demanding audience. Their work is largely
routinized, so that what they preach and what they do are two separate
things.

In addition, they too confront the question of meaning. If, for
football players, meaning is impersonalized and lies outside the system, for the rock star, it is personalized and lies within the individual.
However, the result is the same—a sense of personal loss. For as *every*
conceivable personal experience becomes meaningful, *no* individual
experience remains very meaningful. As a result, the lives of rock stars
are often characterized by a constant search for meaning derived from
novel or more intense experiences. Rock performers are noted for
dying from overdoses of drugs, which are taken either to produce
heightened states of consciousness, or at least to provide a temporary
escape from the intolerability of what becomes a meaningless everyday
existence.

The difficulties that beset both football players and rock stars as
they try to act out only one of the two models are largely related to lack
of flexibility. There are times when social needs are paramount, and
times when the individual must act on his own needs. Further, meaning is located neither wholly within an external system nor wholly
within the individual, but in the interplay between the two. Taken
together, the two models provide the actor with flexible guidelines.
Futher, because the two models share legitimacy under the same success umbrella, the individual need never feel he is acting inconsis-
tently as he switches back and forth between them. And because the
concept of success is articulated with universal law, both the individual
and society recognize that his actions are at all times consonant (unless
he applies the wrong success model to the situation) with the higher
goal, the management of human affairs according to the rules of the
universe. That indeed is success.

In this paper, we have attempted to describe how two success
models, the traditional and the creative, are enacted and grounded as
truth in two performance modes, football games and rock concerts. We
have also examined the question of why American culture contains two

radically different success models. However, we have barely scratched the surface, and have left untouched a host of questions, among the most important of which is: What are the criteria individuals use in deciding which success model to apply to which life situation? At this point, we simply do not know.

Notes

We wish to thank the many American informants who patiently discussed football, rock, and success with us. We are also grateful to W. Arens, Richard Feinberg, Julia Hecht, and Michael Moffatt for their thoughtful comments on an earlier draft of the paper.

1. Success models thus propose behavioral guidelines that are only indirectly linked to the universal laws. However, the symbolism of love maintains the illusion of a direct linkage.

2. Huber notes that competition has been a continual problem for traditional success-model writers. They play down interpersonal competition, preferring the view that the actor competes with himself (i.e., with his baser desires) to achieve. He also notes that Social Darwinism has only rarely been advocated by traditional success-model writers precisely because its dog-eat-dog tenets conflict with the Christian love ethic (1971).

References

Cohn, Nik, 1974, *Rock Dreams*. New York: Popular Library.

Fiske, Shirley, 1975, "Pigskin Review: An American Initiation." In Michael A. Rynkiewich and James R. Spradley, eds. *The Nacirema: Readings on American Culture*. Boston: Little, Brown.

Geertz, Clifford, 1966, "Religion as a cultural System." In M. Banton. ed., *Anthropological Approaches to the Study of Religion*. London: Tavistock.

Huber, Richard M., 1971, *The American Idea of Success*. New York: McGraw-Hill.

Leibovitz, Annie, ed., 1973, *Shooting Stars: The Rolling Stone Book of Portraits*. San Francisco: Straight Arrow Books.

Shaw, Bernard, 1961, *The Millionairess*. London: Penguin.

Shaw, Gary, 1972, *Meat on the Hoof*. New York: Dell.

Stone, W. Clement, 1962, *The Success System that Never Fails*. Englewood Cliffs, N.J.: Prentice-Hall.

POKER
AND THE
AMERICAN DREAM
REX L. JONES

Poker is an American game. Its orgins, style of play, and language are all American. The draw poker clubs of Gardena in southern California recognize this fact. An advertising brochure of one of the clubs states:

> Poker is America's favorite card game. 70 million adults play cards and some 47 million prefer poker. Poker is as American as baseball and hotdogs. Many of our most famous Presidents were poker enthusiasts.

Poker is a pure expression of the American dream. Embodied in the action of the game is the ever-present notion that anyone with skill, individual initiative, patience, foresight, and a little luck can easily make the leap from rags to riches. In a recent article entitled, "Who Dealt This Mess?" Barry Golson says that poker "is as perfect a microcosm as we have of the way a free-enterprise system is *supposed* to work, except that the rich don't necessarily get richer." He goes on to say that "in a limit game . . . a grocery clerk can humiliate an oil tycoon through sheer bravado—the object being, without exception, to bankrupt the bastard across the table" (1974: 112).

Poker is an expression of the American dream in many other ways. We recognize the person who has achieved the Amercan dream by conspicuous consumption. A house, a car, a color TV, a pocket full of credit cards, and a politician in the closet are some of the indications of success. In poker, the "winner" is easily recognized by diamonds, stickpins, car, clothes, bankroll, and the hangers-on who flank him. He exudes rugged individualism—the winner at poker is his own man.

In the realization of the American dream, the arena is the system of free enterprise, where everyone has an equal chance; in the poker game, the arena is a system of free play, where all begin on equal footing. In the American dream, society is classless, anyone can play; it is the same with poker. In the American dream, the way to the top is up to you and you alone; in poker, too, winning is solely an individual effort. In the American dream, the winner takes all; in poker, there is no such thing as sharing the spoils.

The American dream and the game of poker thus have much in common. The latter is the microcosm of the former. In Gardena, this melodrama is reenacted every day from 9 A.M. until 5 A.M. the next day. Most of the people who participate are the senior citizens of America—the retired, and the widowed, or that element of our society for whom the American dream has indeed become a living nightmare, because old age and retirement have made its realization next to impossible.

Daily, elderly men, living on their pensions and savings, and elderly women, living on inheritances and insurance premiums of their deceased husbands, frequent the poker clubs, often in shared taxis or cars, to pursue their vision of the American dream. They meet their friends, share stories of winning and losing, compare notes on racing forms, watch TV, eat, drink, and participate in the "action" with people from all walks of life. Small businessmen, bartenders, teachers, construction workers, doctors, students, hustlers, prostitutes, the unemployed, and tourists intermingle with the senior citizens, who all too often in our society are confined to the sterility of old-age homes or the loneliness of their rooms.

In Gardena, the poker clubs may be many things to many people, but to the aged they are—as expressed to me by an 83-year-old woman—a "godsend." In the clubs their lives attain new meaning. In Gardena, few discuss their aches and pains or their imminent and inevitable deaths. The talk centers around poker and especially winning, which few if any are able to do consistently. No matter, there is always hope, and such hope is justified every day, when a few hit a big win. Winnings are remembered for years; losses are forgotten the next day. In the process, however, the American dream is perpetuated through poker play, and even the old can participate in the myth.

POKER PLAYING IN SOUTHERN CALIFORNIA

In California there are over 400 licensed and legalized draw-poker clubs. In Gardena, a sprawling suburb of about 50,000 people, located 10 miles south of downtown Los Angeles, poker is the major industry. The poker club payrolls amount to around $5 million annually. Thousands of southern Californians are attracted to its six poker parlors every year, most of them regular players. The Gardena clubs are the largest and best equipped of any of the California draw poker clubs.

Each club is limited, by city law, to thirty-five tables; each table seats a maximum of eight players. In addition to the card tables, each club features a restaurant, lounge, and one or more color TV rooms. The restaurants serve decent food with diversified menus, at relatively low prices. Many serve weekly specials and buffets that attract hundreds of people who never sit at the poker tables. The clubs are tastefully decorated, by California standards, well lit, and provide free parking. They are located near major freeway systems and are therefore easily accessible to motor-crazed southern Californians.

Draw poker is still the number one attraction. In Gardena's clubs, as in most poker parlors in California, the house has no interest in the stakes of the games. The house provides the tables, cards, chips, game supervision, and other services, but the deal rotates among the players. Each player pays a "collection" to the house at the end of each half-hour of play, the amount being determined by the stakes of the table. The lower the stakes, the less the collection. The house, then, essentially rents its services to those who wish to play poker. The collection, however, is no minor variable in terms of winning and losing.

Because of the collection at the end of each half-hour, a low-stakes game is a death wish. It took me some 1000 hours of poker playing to figure out this mathematical formula. In a game of, let's say, $1.00/$2.00 draw, the collection is $1.25 each half-hour. The "buy in," or the stakes that you are required to place in front of you on the table, is $10.00. If all eight players at the table are of equal skill, and if at the end of 4 hours of play no player has won or lost at the card play, there will be no money on the table. Each and every player will be broke. Collectively, it costs $80.00 for 4 hours of play. The rent is not cheap.

As one moves to a higher-stakes game, the collection increases, but it increases disproportionately to the stakes of the game. For example, at a $10/$20 low draw game, the collection is $3.00 per half-hour. Collectively, at the end of 4 hours of play, it costs $192.00 per table to play. But the buy-in at $10/$20 low draw is $100.00. It would take from 16 to 17 hours, everything being equal, for the players at the table to go broke.

What this means for the regular players at Gardena is quite simple. Those who regularly play the low-stakes game, *even if they win at cards consistently,* will find it next to impossible to "beat the collection." They will lose money, not to the other players, but to the house. In 1970, I played regularly for 6 months in low-stakes games at Gardena, usually 1/2 high draw or 2/4 low draw. I played on the average of 50 hours a week, or a total of 1500 hours. It cost me in collection fees an average of $3.00 per hour, or a total for 6 months of some $4,500. In tabulating the amount of money I spent at Gardena during that 6-month period, I estimate expenses of $2000. Out of that $2000 also came my food, transportation, and such other things as cigarettes and drinks. Any way I calculated it, I had won at cards. I estimate my winnings at close to $3000, yet my bank account was some $2000 short. What happened to the money? It went to the house.

I am convinced that this happens to every regular player at Gardena in low stakes games.[1] This is substantiated by hundreds of interviews with people who play poker at Gardena and are aware that the house wins in the end. How else could the clubs meet a $5 million annual payroll, pay Gardena taxes, and also make a profit?

Who Plays Poker at Gardena?

As indicated, the majority of the regular players are senior citizens. Surveys of five clubs at different intervals of the day and week during the summer of 1974 revealed some of the following statistics: Out of a total sample of 1473 people at the tables, 789 (53 percent) were over 60 years of age. Of the total sample, 1089 (74 percent) were men and 384 (26 percent) were women. Of the men, 503 (46 percent) were over 60, and of the women, 286 (74 percent) were over 60 (see Appendix A). These figures indicate that the majority of players are of retirement age. Three-fourths of all women who play are at the retirement age and probably either widowed or playing their pensions or inheritances.

The surveys were backed up by some 3000 hours of participant observation at the tables over a period of five years. During that time, I have informally interviewed hundreds of regular players, most of whom indicated to me that they were retired or living on pensions, inheritances, or savings.[2]

Furthermore, the majority of the aged and retired play low-stakes games. I estimate roughly three-fourths or more.[3] The reasons are simple. They are generally unable to afford the potential losses of high-stakes games, which at any given period of play can run into several hundred dollars or more.

In both formal and informal interview situations and during the course of hours of play, I found that consistent winners are few, probably less than 2 percent, and are of a certain type.[4] They are invariably young (between 21 and 35 years of age), male, and single.[5] These data correspond roughly to another study of poker playing in northern California by Martinez and LaFranchi (1972, 1974), who claim that the consistent winners were single or divorced, male, and younger than most of the other players. In that study, they also indicated that less than 10 percent of the players were consistent winners. They described the remainder as "break-evens," "losers," or "action players." I feel that a similar situation exists in Gardena, with one exception. In the Martinez-LaFranchi study there is no mention or analysis of the variable of the house collection. The majority of Gardena players probably fall into the area of "break-evens" or "losers" in terms of the card play, but I am convinced that well over 90 percent of all people who play poker regularly in the Gardena clubs lose money, regardless of their card play.[6] I would add only one variable to Martinez and LaFranchi's description of the consistent winner, and that is that he will probably be found in the high-stakes games, especially $10/$20 draw.

The conclusion to my study is that the senior citizens who regularly play poker at Gardena lose money in one way or another. They spend their pensions or savings in order to frequent the clubs. The amount they lose is consistent with their income. The club owners recognize this, implicitly if not explicitly. As an example, last summer I played frequently at a $5/$10 low-draw game with a woman who was 76 years old and consistently lost money. In such a game, the losses can be heavy. An average win at a period of play in that game will range from $150 to $300. An average loss will amount to the same or more depending on the player. This woman knew this, because she had played the game in Gardena, in the same club, for over 20 years. She first began playing in the 1950s after moving to California from New York with her husband. Her husband, a successful businessman, died shortly after the move, leaving her with a fairly large income. After a period of boredom and loneliness, the woman soon discovered poker at Gardena, through a friend. Because she had the money, she rapidly moved to the high-stakes games, where the action was faster and more to her liking. During her play, she talked constantly, and frequently claimed that she had paid for the entire west wing of the club through collections over the years. She said that last year she had cashed $20,000 in checks at the cashier's window. At the end of the year, the owner of the club invited her into his office for a personal conference, and begged her to play at a lower-stakes game where she would not lose so much money. She refused, and said, "What else have I got to do with my money? Go on a goddamned world cruise with a bunch of old ladies? I'd rather lose it at poker!"

To the club owner, it matters little whether such people play low- or high-stakes games. The difference in the collection is not so great. What matters is keeping his customers happy and playing, re-gardless of their losses or winnings.[7] He feared that the woman might go broke, or anger the other players by creating disturbances over her losses, none of which were to his advantage. Thus, the conference was held to "help her out." The important thing was to keep her playing, and playing happily.

Why Poker Playing at Gardena?

As I have maintained, the people who play poker at Gardena are mostly senior citizens, and most of them lose money on a regular basis. The "diamond-studded woman" of Gardena who coldly calculates her cards and shrewdly takes in her winnings, as described by Jack Richardson (1974) in a recent *Playboy* article, is a rarity, if not a myth. The player you are most likely to find across the table from you is an elderly male in wrinkled slacks and a $5.00 sport shirt, losing his pension, or an elderly female with a wig and make-up, losing her inheritance or savings.

It is my contention that the aged and retired play poker in Gardena for social and recreational reasons. They are reliving the American dream, which gives meaning to their lives. Poker functions to make them young again.

The Gardena clubs take the place of home life for the aged. They function quite simply as old-age homes, but offer a more exciting and stimulating environment than do regular institutions for the aged in our society. The clubs, unlike old-age homes, are not places to go and die but places to go and live. Here the aged, the retired, and the widowed are able to interact on a one-to-one basis with thousands of young people, who frequent the clubs simply to play cards. Here the regulars meet tourists from all over the United States and Canada. They meet and interact with people from all walks of life. The clubs offer something more to the regulars than the loneliness and passivity of old-age homes, where people spend most of their time thinking about illness, misfortune, and death. Such discussions are out of place in Gardena.

CONCLUSION

Studies of this kind are of extreme importance to sociologists and anthropologists interested in American culture and behavior. Considering the importance of this pastime to most Americans, we should be able to add new dimensions to studies of gambling and gamblers. In the past, this area of human behavior has been left to psychologists such as Bergler (1957), who insist on describing the gambler as "compulsive" or a "psychopath." There are sociological reasons for gambling. In many instances it is a form of recreation or play (Stone, 1972), not a compulsive neurotic search for the affections of one's father or mother. Zola (1964: 247), citing studies by psychologists (Hunter and Bruner, 1928; Morris, 1957) claims that there is no convincing evidence on any number of psychological dimensions to indicate that gamblers differ significantly from nongamblers in personality characteristics. However, his studies (1964) and a select few by other sociologists (Devereaux, 1949; Carlson, 1939) show that there are significant sociological reasons that people gamble. Frequently, gambling as described by Zola (1964: 259) is a functional social activity that creates "rationality," "order," and "meaning" in the lives of alienated, frustrated, and predetermined failures. Poker playing in Gardena serves such a positive function for the aged and retired who are outside the mainstream of American social life. As one 83-year-old woman put it at the end of an interview in which she systematically pointed out the evils and absurdities of playing poker at Gardena, "Son, if they closed Gardena tomorrow, I would die."

Appendix

Head Count of Poker Players by Sex and Age in Five Different Clubs on Five Separate Days of the Week

	Club A	Club B	Club C	Club D	Club E
Total	271	400	245	234	323
Men	195	342	202	158	192
percent	(68)	(83)	(83)	(64)	(60)
Women	76	58	43	76	131
percent	(32)	(17)	(17)	(36)	(40)
Men over 60	107	138	81	69	108
percent	(55)	(41)	(41)	(44)	(56)
Women over 60	70	49	36	50	81
percent	(92)	(84)	(64)	(65)	(62)

Total Head Count of 5 Clubs: —1473 people
1089 (74 percent) men
384 (26 percent) women
503 (46 percent) men over 60
286 (74 percent) women over 60

The numbers in the table were obtained by walking through the play-area and counting the men and women. I then repeated the walk, noting the women over 65. (In the chart, I indicate "over 60" to allow five years' difference in "guessing age".) I then did the same for men.

Although I give only the figures for 5 clubs on 5 different days, I did this 15 times in 5 different clubs (3 times each), to act as a check on my figures. The figures varied, of course, but the percentages of male to female and ages did not vary a great deal.

As a further check on my guessing of ages, I had an independent observer (an anthropologist friend of mine) do a similar head count in one evening of play. Our figures tallied very closely. Thus, although the ages are guesswork, I feel that the above checks and years of experience in Gardena make them fairly accurate guesses.

Notes

1. Such statements are extremely difficult to substantiate accurately, since players regularly talk of their winnings but are more reluctant to discuss their losses, especially over long periods of time. But based on close contact with hundreds of regular players in low-stakes games, I never came across an individual who admitted to being a consistent winner in those games. They all had excuses for losing, but generally, reluctantly admitted that the house collection was indeed the real problem.

In Gardena, the house collection is presented in such a way as to make the players believe that it is a necessary part of playing poker. Next to the cashier is a sign that reads something like: "For tax purposes, law in the city of Gardena requires each player to pay his collection on demand." This is to instill in the players the idea that most of the collection goes to the city of Gardena, rather than to the owner of the clubs. Failure to pay, therefore, makes you a tax fraud. Few are fooled by this gambit, however, and the most frequent utterance in Gardena is that "Nobody but the house wins."

2. In addition to informal interviews and acquaintances, I conducted twenty-five formal interviews with a cross section of regulars in the summer of 1974. Of all those interviewed who were over 60 (except one), all were living on either a pension or an inheritance, usually small.

3. This figure is difficult to pin down in Gardena, since the tables change personnel so frequently. It is estimated on the basis of hours of play, both in low- and high-stakes games, and comments by players themselves.

4. Two percent is an estimate, also. But of all my experience, in both playing and interview situations, I encountered only about six or eight admitted consistent winners. Four of these were "house players" (see footnote 7). All played either $10/$20 high draw or $10/$20 low "blind."

5. All admitted winners were male. I suspected one or two females of being winners who played in high-stakes games, but they would not discuss this matter.

6. This estimate is based both on my own study and that of Martinez and LaFranchi (1972, 1974).

7. The house even employs house-players to keep the games moving. The house-player usually is paid a daily wage to fill in at short tables. To be a house-player one must risk his own money at the tables, and before employment, put up a thousand dollars in the house bank. Most consistent winners I encountered were house-players.

References

Bergler, E., 1957, *The Psychology of Gambling*. New York: Hill & Wang.
Carlson, G. C., 1939, "Number Gambling—A Study of a Culture Complex." Unpublished Ph.D. dissertation, University of Michigan.
Devereaux, E. C., Jr., 1949, "Gambling and the Social Structure: A Sociological Study of Lotteries and Horse Racing in Contemporary America."

Unpublished Ph.D. dissertation, Harvard.

Golson, B., 1974, "Who Dealt This Mess?" *Playboy,* November, p. 110.

Hunter, J. and A. Bruner, 1928, "Emotional Outlets of Gamblers." *Journal of Abnormal Psychology,* 23:38-39.

Martinez, T. H. and R. LaFranchi, 1972, "Why People Play Poker." In G. P. Stone, ed. *Games, Sport and Power.* Pp. 55-73. New Brunswick, N.J.: Dutton.

—1974, "What Kind of Poker Player are You?" *Gambling Quarterly* (summer): 23, 38, 39.

Morris, R. P., 1957, "An Exploratory Study of Some Personality Characteristics of Gamblers." *Journal of Clinical Psychology* 13: 191-193.

Richardson, Jack, 1974, "Coming Down in Gardena." *Playboy,* November, p. 114.

Stone, G. P., ed., 1972, *Games, Sport and Power.* New Brunswick, N.J.: Dutton.

Zola, Irving R., 1964, "Observations on Gambling in a Lower-class Setting." In Harvard S. Becker, ed., *Perspectives on Deviance: The Other Side.* Pp. 247-260. London: Collier-Macmillan.

Ivan Karp is a social anthropologist interested in studies of cosmology, ritual, social organization, and change. A particular interest of his is in socially defined situations which are different from the contexts of everyday life, such as ritual drama and play.

Marx Brothers movies represent a form of play that has affinities with ritual as well. Play and ritual are not entirely the same, but our society draws a rigid boundary between the two that is not entirely found elsewhere.

Examining the movies of the Marx Brothers as if they were ritual helps us to understand how the domains of play and ritual overlap and how we have drawn an artificial boundary between them in our own world. Thus this paper is an exercise in relating ritual to play, especially those performances that anthropologists have called "rituals of rebellion" which display significant reversals of the distribution of power. The lowly exercise authority over the high, and the high are brought to the level of the low. On the one hand, the paper shows that a cultural form or popular art can be examined in terms of an anthropological literature devoted to "tribal" rituals. On the other hand, the paper uses a specific case study to demonstrate that the literature on rituals of rebellion is a specific instance of a more general form in which a fundamental human problem is revealed, one that takes different form in different societies. It has been argued that in order for society to exist individuals must give up some of their freedom, that freely acting individuals would create a disorded anarchy in which, in the words of the political philosopher Thomas Hobbes, the life of

*man would be "nasty, brutish and short." Society,
then, exercises a tyranny over the individual. This
experience of the tyranny of form over life is
presented in potentially subversive media, such
as art and ritual. The Marx Brothers, in their
movies, express an attitude of rebellion towards
this tyranny.*

GOOD MARX FOR THE ANTHROPOLOGIST
Structure and Anti-Structure in "Duck Soup"
IVAN KARP

It might strike the reader as a dubious exercise but I intend to take some of the concepts developed in the study of ritual in non-Western societies and apply them to the movie *Duck Soup*. The intention is to make sense out of apparent nonsense. Ritual, in this sense, does not necessarily refer to religious action—behavior directed toward "non-empirical beings."[1] Thus I use a definition that regards ritual as an aspect of social behavior directed toward making statements about how the actor "thinks and feels about . . . [social] relationships and about the natural and social environments in which they occur" (Turner, 1969: 6). Some social behavior is more oriented to saying things than to getting things done, although there are elements of both in everything that people do. Social behavior that is predominantly expressive (oriented to saying things) and performed on special occasions is called "ritual" by anthropologists.[2] The analysis of the meaning of behavior on these occasions draws connections between what the ritual expresses and other dimensions of social life or other situations in which the actors might find themselves.

There is not always a direct relationship between what is expressed and what the ritual refers to. In fact, most anthropologists who are interested in understanding rituals agree that if something can be expressed directly, then there is little reason for it to be expressed in a ritual format. If there is one aspect of ritual that may be referred to as the "function" of ritual, it is that it allows for the expression of what is otherwise inexpressible. This is why anthropologists often fail to obtain significant results from questioning people about their rituals. How can they explain what they are otherwise not allowed to say or cannot say except through ritual? Thus it is not so paradoxical that the best informants for anthropologists are often persons who are marginal to their own society and, as a consequence, are more involved in questioning the social conditions of their existence.[3]

One anthropologist whose work has been very influential in this regard is V. W. Turner, who in a series of essays and monographs on the Ndembu of Zambia has examined the relationship between what is expressed in ritual and the experiences of the actors—particularly to their social and personal conflicts (1967, 1968, 1969). In the course of his analysis, Turner has evolved the concept of "anti-structure," which he uses to examine the relationship of what is expressed in ritual to the structure of society, and also to explain why ritual helps to resolve or at least mediate conflicts in which participants are involved. My concern however is not with conflict resolution or mediation; instead I want to use the concept of anti-structure to describe *Duck Soup*. This is done in order to demonstrate that anti-structure is a useful analytical tool for examining the interrelations among roles played by actors (in the theatrical sense) on some expressive occasions, such as in movies, and the roles played by actors (in the social sense) on formal and public occasions during which the hierarchy of etiquette prevails. Thus, this is a modest attempt at academic imperialism since I am convinced that there are as yet no theoretical reasons for asserting that there are substantial differences between what is called a "primitive ritual" and an expressive occasion such as a movie.

Turner's conception of anti-structure derives from the theoretical position which views social structure as a system of constraints applied to social persons to coerce them to behave in ways antithetical to their immediate self-interests.[4] Structure is not the only aspect of society that merits description, however. For Turner, structure can only be effective as a system of constraints because the persons involved alternate their participation in structure with occasions that are anti-structural in nature and meaning. Turner views the alternation of structure and anti-structure as the major unanalyzed aspect in the study of society. I shall not be concerned here with the relation of anti-structure and structure to social stability and change. Rather, I want to use Turner's important insight that there are in many societies occa-

sions reserved for the expression of attitudes, opinions, and feelings
that are not tolerated in the etiquette of other, and especially public,
occasions. The importance of these ritual expressions of anti-structure
is that these publicly intolerable attitudes are positively valued on
ritual occasions instead of being negatively sanctioned. Hence, the
expression of anti-structure bears a dialetical relationship to the constraints imposed on other, more structural, occasions.

> Society (*societas*) seems to be a process rather than a thing—a dialetical
> process with successive phases of structure and communitas. There
> would seem to be—if one can use such a controversial term—a human
> "need" to participate in both modalities. Persons starved of one in their
> functional day-to-day activities seek it in ritual liminality. The structur-
> ally inferior aspire to symbolic structural superiority in ritual; the struc-
> turally superior aspire to symbolic communitas and undergo penance to
> achieve it. (1969: 203)

It might be added that Turner's "dialectics" differs from classical
Hegelian-Marxian dialectics in that the alternation of structure and
anti-structure does not imply a *transcendence* of one by the other. In
Turner's formulation structure and anti-structure chase each other in a
perpetual equilibrium.

In his most recent essay on this topic Turner (1974) distinguishes
"liminality" and "communitas" as the two dimensions of anti-structure.
Liminality is typically found during transition rituals, in which persons
move from one identity to another. In these instances individuals are
stripped of one identity and before they assume another, they exist in a
state that is "betwixt and between." Their liminal state expresses a
contravention of the structure without an assertion of other social possibilities. Communitas is expressed during liminal states. It is the ritual
opposite of structure in that it unites persons whom structure separates
in terms of social distance, and exists in continual tension with structure
at all levels of organization (1974: 274-275). The form that communitas
might take is related to but not determined by the structure of the
society in which the ritual is embedded. Turner stresses the *dialectical*
and *necessary* relationship between structure and communitas or,
more generally, structure and anti-structure.

In what follows below I describe the relationships expressed by a
set of characters in the Marx Brothers' classic film *Duck Soup* to the
structural relationships expressed by the etiquette of public occasions.
I trust that if the following analysis does not illuminate the reader's
understanding of the Marx Brothers' movies, it will not lessen his
enjoyment of them. It hasn't mine.

Duck Soup is an appropriate vehicle for analysis because it is
generally acknowledged as the zenith of the Marx Brothers' art. However, it was not a commercial success and their contract with

Paramount Studios was not renewed after this film. This initiated the Marx Brothers' sad artistic decline—guided intially by the capable but crass Irving Thalberg (Adamson, 1973). The film was created in order for the Marx Brothers to express their artistic personalities without the regard found in many of their earlier films for plot constraints or the conventions of the Broadway or vaudeville stage. Therefore, in *Duck Soup* we have the Marx Brothers at their best and in a vehicle that expresses what is most distinctive about them.

For those who may be unfamiliar with the film's plot, I will present a brief synopsis, which I preface with the warning that plots are the creatures of structure. Consequently, to pay too much attention to twists of plot in a vehicle of anti-structure such as *Duck Soup* is to refuse to enter into the spirit of the occasion. First, the title. Unsubstantiated rumor has it that the title refers to the Marx Brothers' opinion of the quality of the food at the Paramount dining room—Duck Soup! Groucho has another explanation: "Take two turkeys, one goose, four cabbages, but no duck, and mix them together. After one taste, you'll duck soup the rest of your life" (Adamson, 1973: 224). Back to the plot. The imaginary country of Fredonia is in the midst of a financial crisis. The crisis is resolved by Mrs. Teasdale (played by Margaret Dumont), the wealthy widow of a former prime minister. Her price is to have her candidate installed as chief of state. The new prime minister, Rufus T. Firefly (played by Groucho Marx), appears to be installed at a grand ball where his first words as prime minister are, "take a card." His first official act is to dictate a letter to his dentist. He then sings a song about the policies he will follow in office. The refrain goes: "If any form of pleasure is exhibited, report it to me and it will be prohibited." A recent commentary on the film tells us:

> the only difference between him and any other head of state is that coming from his mouth it sounds funny. Disrespect for crowned heads is what we're all set to see Groucho perform, but he executes the most ignoble sacrilege on the whole condition of sovereignty just by taking office. . . . He cheerfully proclaims he'll accept all the power due his office and none of the responsibility, and it gets a rise out of the people instead of an uprising. His conversation about Margaret Dumont's husband (who . . . [he says] died of a surfeit of Margaret Dumont) gets the same response out of her: Groucho is a bald-faced opportunist and makes no bones about it. He is the ideal ruler. (Adamson, 1973: 227).

While the plot gets far more complicated, it doesn't make any better sense. Groucho gets into a series of disputes with Ambassador Trentino of the neighboring country of Sylvania who is after Mrs. Teasdale's money. Somehow the fights lead to a declaration of war between the two countries. The manifest reason is a contest of honor between Groucho-Firefly and Trentino that would put the fiercest Mediterranean countryman to shame. Chico (under the nom de guerre of Chicolini) and Harpo (who doesn't have a name at all)[5] are spies for Trentino and, when not stealing plans of war, they are working for Groucho and vending peanuts. Finally the spies are caught, but their trial—made into a travesty by Chico and the worst puns anyone has ever heard—is interrupted by war with Sylvania, Ambassador Trentino's country. The events of this particular conflict are not reducible to mere words. Fredonia wins after Trentino is caught in the door of a house in which the Marx Brothers are blockaded. They pelt him with fruit until he surrenders. The victory stirs Mrs. Teasdale to break into the national anthem of Fredonia; so the Marx Brothers pelt *her* with fruit. We aren't allowed to stay around long enough to discover if she surrenders.

Plot takes us exactly where the movie intended—nowhere. In the world of anti-structure a logical, linear progression has no particular place. There must be a beginning and an end in order to leave and return to structure again, but it matters little if we begin at the middle and end before the beginning. If sense is not to be made of the film at the level of a sequence of events, it must be found at another level. Otherwise audiences would not still be overcome with hysteria by this film 40 years after it was made. I suggest that the level at which sense is to be found is in the logic of social relations and in the relationship of that logic to the audience's experience of the participation in social relationships having a similar structural pattern.[6] In pursuing this mode of analysis I am not departing in any way from the conventional anthropological analysis of ritual. Social anthropologists from Van Gennep (1960) on have examined the patterns of transformations that the normative content of social relationships undergo on ritual occasions. Studies of ritually privileged license and obscenity bear this out.

The pivot of most of the Marx Brothers' movies is the relationship between Groucho and those he victimizes. They are, by and large, persons in social positions that demand respect and deference, and are naturally offended when they receive less than what they require as their social due. Ambassador Trentino of *Duck Soup,* or Herman Gottlieb, the pompous and self-satisfied manager of the New York Opera from *A Night at the Opera,* are good examples of this type, but the ubiquitous Margaret Dumont, the archetype of the dowager matron, provides us with the purest representative of the kind. There is nothing especially mean or malicious or even particularly self-seeking about Mrs. Teasdale and the other dowagers that Margaret Dumont usually plays. She is merely a pompous woman (often a widow) who either represents or wants to represent the pinnacle of social prestige. She is always wealthy and willing to use her wealth for philanthropic purposes—as she understands them. Groucho, on the other hand, is willing to use her. She is destined to be Groucho's foil. His intention is to flatter her, seduce her, and marry her in order to enjoy her wealth. His exchanges with her start out with Groucho expressing admiration for her beauty, figure, intelligence, culture, or whatever else comes to mind. Groucho's trouble is that he can't keep *his* mind on the job at hand. His distaste for Dumont always gets the better of him, and he winds up expressing his genuine and very funny opinion of her. In *Duck Soup* he impugns her honor, insults her figure, portrays her as overcome by uncontrollable sexual desire, and implies that she drove her husband to his death. Otherwise they get on fine.

We might conclude that Groucho is not polite to her. And that is precisely what strikes us as particularly funny about their relationship. Proper behavior in a given situation is very important to the characters that Margaret Dumont plays. She stresses both for herself and the people around her proper dress, proper demeanor, and proper etiquette. The formal garden party and the inaugural ball are her milieu in *Duck Soup*. Even in her boudoir she presents us with a formally and impeccably well dressed presence. Her major concern appears to be that the social forms are maintained; and she directs a sense of outrage at persons who do not defer to and recognize the importance of such socially eminent persons as ambassadors and cabinet ministers. She is the type of character who remains a stock figure in satires, from Gilbert and Sullivan's *The Mikado* (which has a good deal in common with *Duck Soup*) on to the present.

Because of her emphasis on the structural (i.e., public) characteristics of individuals rather than on their personal qualities, she is a stifling and constraining presence. The very existence of Groucho (not to mention what he says and does to her) liberates the audience from Margaret Dumont. In classical structuralist fashion the differences between Rufus T. Firefly as portrayed by Groucho and Mrs. Teasdale as portrayed by Margaret Dumont can be represented through a series of oppositions.

Where Teasdale is always impeccably tailored, Firefly is always dressed in an ill-fitting outfit. Both Mrs. Teasdale and Firefly are aware of the rules of etiquette but while she is concerned with upholding the rules of conventional morality, Firefly pokes fun at the people who live by the rules and respond emotionally to their violations. Thus, the net effect of the Groucho-Dumont opposition or the Firefly-Teasdale opposition (they amount to the same thing) is to provide the audience with a spectacular and ongoing relationship of continual status reversal. By victimizing her on the basis of publicly displaying her disconcerting (for her) personal characteristics, her claims to superiority are turned to a position of social inferiority. The relationship is based on Mrs. Teasdale's claims about her superior status vis-a-vis the rest of the world (including Firefly). Firefly exploits those claims by providing information and attitudes that poke fun, often cruel fun, at the pretensions of Teasdale and most of the people he is surrounded by. The audience participates in what becomes the disruption of claims to deference on public occasions. The audience is able, in fact willing, to participate because these claims are based on the assumption that the norms of social behavior express differences of quality between the actors. Firefly expresses what many of the audience will have felt many times but had been forced to repress—that their definition of the situation does not merit the assumption of inequality, which they see themselves as forced to acknowledge and legitimize on public occasions.

Firefly and Teasdale represent an important starting point for this analysis. Other dimensions are to be found in the characters played by Chico and Harpo. Chico's character is called, with startling originality, Chicolini while Harpo's character has no name, or at least it is not revealed to the audience.

Chicolini is, as with all the characters Chico plays, an immigrant. He wears funny clothes, talks with an accent, and works at what are almost archetypically immigrant occupations. In *Duck Soup* he runs a combination peanut and hotdog stand and supplements his income with a little espionage on the side. If he were an organ grinder and had a monkey on a string, I don't think we would be surprised. But this is no immigrant made for poking fun at. Although he represents the image of the greenhorn so dear to vaudeville and later burlesque comedians, he is not the one who is taken in and fleeced. The fleecing, with an appropriately mixed metaphor, is on the other foot. Chico's main contribution to the Marx Brothers' movies in general, and *Duck Soup* in particular, is through a series of outrageous puns. His wit makes no more linear sense than Groucho's or Harpo's. The major difference is that, while Groucho's humor is aimed at deflating pomposity, Chico's humor is aimed at taking advantage of his victim's image of Chico as ignorant and gullible. In *Duck Soup* Chicolini plays with that image by perpetrating on us a series of puns and by taking advantage of the same people that Firefly mocks. Consider the following dialogue:

The Shadow

Trentino: Oh! Now, Chicolini, I want a full detailed report of your investigation.

Chico: All right, I tell you. Monday we watch-a Firefly's house, but he no come out. He wasn't home. Tuesday we go to the ball game, but he fool us. He no show up. Wednesday he go to the ball game, and we fool him. We no show up. Thursday was a doubleheader. Nobody show up. Friday it rained all day. There was no ball game, so we stayed home and we listened to it over the radio.

Trentino: Then you didn't shadow Firefly?

Chico: Oh, sure we shadow Firefly. We shadow him all day.

Trentino: But what day was that?

Chico: Shadowday! Hahaha. Atsa some joke, eh, Boss?
(Adamson, 1973: 227)

or again when Chicolini is on trial for espionage:

The Trial

Groucho: Chicolini, give me a number from one to ten.

Chico: Eleven.

Groucho: Right.

Chico: Now I ask you one. What is it has a trunk, but no key, weighs 2,000 pounds, and lives in the circus?

Prosecutor: That's irrelevant.

Chico: A relephant! Hey, that's the answer! There's a whole lotter elephants in the circus.

Minister: That sort of testimony we can eliminate.

Chico: Atsa fine. I'll take some.

Minister: You'll take *what?*

Chico: Eliminate. A nice cool glass eliminate.

*   *   *   *   *   *

Minister of Finance: Something must be done! War would mean a prohibitive increase in our taxes.

Chico: Hey, I got an uncle lives in Taxes.

Minister of Finance: No, I'm talking about taxes—money, dollars.

Chico: Dollas! That's-a where my uncle lives. Dollas, Taxes!

Minister of Finance: Aww!

(Adamson, 1973: 242-243)

If Groucho inverts the norms and values of the social reality that is accepted by the Teasdales and Trentinos of his world, we may say that Chico has a *tangential* relationship to that same reality. He approaches reality from an oblique angle. Chico, however, does not usually act alone. He is accompanied by Harpo. who presents us with a persona entirely different from Chico and Groucho. *Duck Soup* is Harpo's finest hour. All the innate anarchy and formlessness of his character is expressed in this film. Perhaps his finest scene is during his and Chico's conference with Ambassador Trentino. His voluminous clothes produce an assortment of tools from scissors to a blowtorch used for lighting cigars. He consistently, persistently, and absolutely destroys every premise on which social action can be based until the scene can continue no longer. There is no way that the everyday rationality of the Trentino character can deal with the phenomenon of Harpo.

Even Harpo's appearance and manner deny the categories of

everyday life. He is more than just a stock vaudeville clown figure as he is sometimes interpreted. Immediately, one recognizes that his appearance conveys a remarkable kind of sexual ambiguity. His hair, figure, and face cannot be placed in either of the two sexual categories. Perhaps this is because of his childlike manner. His systematic inarticulateness, his lack of social knowledge, his naivete and polymorphous sexuality (in *Duck Soup* he winds up in bed with a horse after chasing a voluptuous blonde)[7] are all reminiscent of the condition of infancy, or at least the Freudian version of infancy.

For whatever the reason, Harpo is not easily placed into basic and perhaps even universal categories of the social world such as man-woman and child-adult. I suggest that this is because Harpo expresses an attitude to the world that is, to quote Turner, "betwixt and between" the world of structure. Harpo is preeminently a *liminal* figure and as such contradicts the most basic values and distinctions of his and our society. Thus, the figure of Harpo represents for the audience the inversion and obliteration of structure in its most elementary forms.

We have in the Marx Brothers' personae three stock figures from drama and comedy, the flimflammer or con man, the immigrant, and the clown. None is admirable by the standards of our society; they are all marginal to the central concerns of anyone trying to get on in life. What these characters have in common, and what the audience responds to, is that they say *NO* to the application of constraints on behavior to which the rest of their world unthinkingly acquiesces. Of course, their very marginality makes them less liable to the imposition of sanctions. They aren't likely to receive the rewards that everyone else is striving so hard to get. Therefore, they are not obliged to accept the discrepancy between the personal perception of a situation and the acknowledgement of a social norm that is part of the audience's experience of the social world. In the case of Harpo, the audience is given an example of freedom from the constraints imposed on action as a result of being placed by other people into basic social categories such as man-woman or child-adult. With Groucho and Chico, the audience is given an example of freedom from constraints (such as being "nice" or "polite" or "paying attention") that are the necessary baggage that accompanies the achievement of social goals through other people.

In fact, I think this is a major aspect of the appeal of the Marx Brothers. Their characters *express* attitudes to the social world that are coterminous with unexpressed attitudes experienced by large portions of the audiences that have appreciated *Duck Soup* and other Marx Brothers films over the years. This is why so many of the Marx Brothers' best scenes are concerned with public occasions such as balls, parties, trials, and operas. On these occasions the presentation of self is limited to the expression of social rather than personal attributes to a far greater degree than on more intimate occasions. In the Marx Brothers films this ritual separation of persons is stood on its head and the brothers and their audience form an unstructured community united through laughter at the structure. Communitas is to be found in the interaction between the audience and the Marx Brothers. In this sense, anyone who attends a performance of *Duck Soup* is engaging in an action akin to taking part in a ritual. How the person responds is, of course, a matter of personal history and temperament. I cannot help but think, however, that the continuing popularity of this movie is based on its ability to strike deep and responsive chords in the experience of the audience.[8]

I have tried, through the use of the concept of anti-structure, to discover within *Duck Soup* elements that correspond to the experiences of the audience that enable it to respond to the movie. I have tried to show that the social world of the Marx Brothers has structural features in common with that of the audience. Instead of viewing *Duck Soup* as an entity in itself, I have stressed a relationship between what is expressed in the film and the social experience of the actors. This relationship demonstrates that anti-structure is not chaotic and formless: it derives its form and meaning from structure.[9] In the case, for example, of Groucho and Margaret Dumont the form of anti-structure is derived from an antithetical relationship of deference expressed in the etiquette of heirarchy. In this sense, anti-structure is like Monica Wilson's (1951) definition of witchcraft as "standardized nightmares" that derive their meaning from tensions found in social relationships (Middleton and Winter, 1963). The difference is that in witchcraft beliefs, the uncertainties that are elements in social action are developed into a moral theory of causation. In Marx Brothers' films the irritants that accompany social action are expressed.

But what happens as a result of the expression of these irritants? Surely, the audience's interpretation of similar experiences has been altered after seeing *Duck Soup,* just as it would have been altered after seeing any movie—no matter how banal. Since this paper has treated *Duck Soup* as a ritual it should conclude with at least some comments on the consequences for the actors of participation in the affair. Although rituals obviously serve to ease social tensions, in each society a ritual must be examined anew before such general conclusions can be reaffirmed. In the case of *Duck Soup* it would be easy but incorrect to suggest that after having seen this movie the audience can rest easier in the face of social inequities. If I did suggest that, the analysis would be dialectical in the sense that Turner uses the notion of dialectics. Instead, I wish to suggest that I find it difficult to imagine how anyone can take *Duck Soup* seriously, in the sense of laughing at what it laughs at, and return to the world of structure and accept with reverence and equanimity the received wisdom of public occasions. The consequence of joining with the Marx Brothers in laughing at structure is to formulate and verify for the moviegoer his private and inchoate experience of the structure, and thus to make that experience an objective, social fact.

In this sense the title of the paper plays on the historical accident of the identicalness of the surnames of Karl Marx and the Marx Brothers. The young Karl Marx called for "*a ruthless criticism of everything existing* . . . ruthless in two senses: The criticism must not be afraid of its own conclusions, nor of conflict with the power that be" (Tucker, 1972: 9, emphasis in original). The Marx Brothers similarly ask us to take nothing for granted, nor to be afraid of our conclusions. Remember Chico's famous line in *Duck Soup*. Groucho has just left Mrs. Teasdale's boudoir. Chico, dressed as Groucho, crawls out from under the bed. Mrs. Teasdale says, "Why, I can't believe my own eyes." "Lady," replies Chico, "Who you gonna believe? Me or your own eyes?"

Notes

I would like to thank Nigel Bolland, Mary Bufwack, David Jacobson, Patricia Karp, and Warren Ramshaw for their penetrating comments on earlier versions of this paper.

1. See Tyler's famous minimal definition of religion, which does not even refer to religion as expressing "ultimate concerns" (Evans-Pritchard, 1965: 25).

2. This approach is illustrated by Leach (1954) and Harris (1957), among others.

3. See Turner's fascinating essay (1967) on just such a person, Muchona, the Hornet.

4. Durkheim's own position of self and society is actually far more radical. For him the self is socially derived and there can be no distinction between self-interests and societal interests. For a discussion of this see Thomas Luckmann's analysis of Durkheim's concept of the self in relation to a sociology of religion (1967).

5. Zimmerman and Goldblatt assert that Harpo is called "Pinky" in *Duck Soup* (1968: 84). I have no such recollection.

6. In a series of works beginning with *The Presentation of Self in Everyday Life*, Erving Goffman has documented the assertion that the private and personal self is allowed little scope for expression on public and formal occasions. See also Meyer Fortes's "Ritual and Office in Tribal Society" in Max Gluckman (1962). In this paper I am taking this portion of the analysis as given. Clearly, I am making a number of assertions about the social experience and state of consciousness of the audience. These are derived partly from my reading of social scientists, such as Goffman, and partly from my own experience. In the absence of empirical evidence that could confirm or deny these assertions, this analysis must be taken as partial and tentative.

7. Is this the same horse whose picture he carried next to his heart in *Animal Crackers?*

8. Here again we confront the problem of assertion about the audience. One reader suggested, for example, that an audience composed largely of college students (as seems to be the case for Marx Brothers fans currently) cannot be analyzed in the same fashion as the earlier, predominantly lower-class audiences of *Duck Soup*. I suggest that the continuing popularity of the

Marx Brothers can be analyzed in terms of continuities in the experience of the audiences. One such continuity might be the marginal relationship to sources of power in our society of both contemporary college students and the 1930s audiences of the Marx Brothers.

9. It only *seems* chaotic and formless to the participants. Anti-structure derives its form through inverting and contravening the structure.

References

Adamson, Joe, 1973, *Groucho, Harpo, Chico and Sometimes Zeppo*. New York: Simon & Schuster.

Evans-Prichard, E. E., 1965, *Theories of Primitive Religion*. London: Oxford University Press.

Gluckman, Max, 1962, *Essays on the Ritual of Social Relations*. Manchester: Manchester University Press.

Goffman, Erving, 1959, *Presentation of Self in Everyday Life*. New York: Anchor.

Harris, Grace, 1957, "Possession 'Hysteria' in a Kenya Tribe." *American Anthropologist* 59: 1046-1066.

Leach, E.R., 1954, *Political Systems of Highland Burma*. London: Oxford University Press.

Luckmann, Thomas, 1967, *The Invisible Religion*. New York: Macmillan.

Middleton, J. and E. H. Winter, eds., 1963, *Witchcraft and Sorcery in East Africa*. London; Routledge & Kegan Paul.

Tucker, R. C., 1972, *The Marx-Engels Reader*. New York: Norton.

Turner, V. W., 1967, *The Forest of Symbols*. Ithaca: Cornell University Press.

—1968, *The Drums of Affliction*. London: Oxford University Press.

—1969, *The Ritual Process*. Chicago: Aldine.

—1974, *Dramas, Fields, and Metaphors*. Ithaca: Cornell University Press.

Van Gennep, A., 1960, *The Rites of Passage*. London: Routledge & Kegan Paul.

Wilson, Monica, 1951, "Witch Beliefs and Social Structure." *American Journal of Sociology* 56: 307-313.

Zimmerman, Paul and Burt Goldblatt, 1968, *The Marx Brothers at the Movies*. New York: New American Library.

Americans tend to dismiss advertisements as a nuisance because they are intended to persuade people to buy. Yet they are carefully crafted products, produced in a way that should, if all goes well, make them acceptable to viewers. I try to show how certain ads and situation comedies draw on similar cultural premises. These premises are crucial to Americans' understanding of what they watch on TV; they may also be important to people's understandings of their own lives. By studying these premises, I feel that we can specify some of the details involved in the construction of a message intended to persuade Americans to laugh or to consider buying a product. We can also learn more about the issues that concern Americans. Since this paper was written, new fads have emerged in the plotting of both comedies and advertisements. I hope that future students of American culture will study these developments to learn whether the parallels noted here between comedies and ads still exist, whether new relations have developed, or whether the differences between the two forms have been increased.

HOMES
AND
HOMEMAKERS
ON AMERICAN TV
JOHN T. KIRKPATRICK

Advertisements and situation comedies are viewed daily by millions of Americans. This paper assumes that these dramatic forms offer valuable insights into contemporary definitions of proper behavior and especially with reference to the role of the "homemaker." The materials studied were initially sorted according to their settings, but it became clear that most kitchen ads, for instance, shared a single organization with laundry room ads, and that the remainder of kitchen ads could be divided into two sets, each having common features with types of ads in other settings. A definitive study of the interaction of setting, characterization, action, and outcome of these ads is beyond the limits of this paper. Rather, the contrast between one type of ad and the situation comedies is stressed in order to bring out features of the dramas found in each.

The evidence from situation comedies comes from a small sample, in which the Norman Lear shows—"All in the Family" and its offspring—are overrepresented. The discussion is not, however, limited to the Lear formula, or even to the fads of the last two years. Such changes as the successive popularity of suburban WASP homes, ethnic homes, and Depression homes for comedy settings should not affect the analysis. The discussion does not, however, account for shows set outside of *family* homes, such as "The Mary Tyler Moore Show."[1]

The data considered here are all presented to an audience of both women and men. Although the ads may be intended to convince women, they are comprehended by far more people than the upwardly mobile young married who are portrayed.

There is a highly general advertising scenario that may be termed the drama of competence. The minimal constituents are a woman, a doubt whether she can handle a problem in homemaking, and a solution to her problem, usually one available in the supermarket. The problem may seem to be a limited, technical one, but we learn that more than the mechanics of, for instance, washing dishes, are involved. A problem of homemaking may threaten the health and identity of the family and raises the issues of whether the woman is "really" a competent homemaker, wife, and mother. Hence when a floor wax protects against scuff marks or when a cereal contains vitamins, these products assert that the woman is truly what she claims to be, mother and homemaker. As the Pillsbury people put it: "Nothin' says lovin' like somethin' from the oven."

The action of the supporting cast is simple. People depend on the heroine's competence, unveil her lack of such, or show her how to gain competence. Each element of the drama may be portrayed in various ways, but there is hardly total free play in the realization of various elements. Some, however, are more amenable to variant forms than others. The product is typically a food or cleansing agent; carpet or bathroom products are inserted into different dramas. The action of cleansing does not determine the drama, for food storage wrappers are advertised just as cleansers are. Mr. Clean, the Man from Glad and others intervene to chase filth and decay from the kitchen and distress from the homemaker.

A rough distinction between dependents and invaders may be drawn on the basis of the threat that characters pose to a homemaker. Dependents include husbands, children, pets and guests. These characters need not simply personify one action of the scenario, and often manifest both dependence and a challenge to competence at the same time. This is obvious, for example, when a child runs into the house, screaming "Mommy!" and tracking mud all over the linoleum. It is obvious that a child is both a dependent and the source of problems of competence. As a result the threat does not need to be realized on the screen. In one floor wax ad the boy doesn't dirty the floor but glides on a translucent surfboard provided by the wax. The problem of competence in this example is voiced by a neighbor, who fails to obtain such splashy effects with her floor wax.

A recent ad for Total cereal concentrates the entire drama in one line. The husband and children have no time to eat more than a bite of breakfast. Mother knows that they need breakfast to do well all day but, as she says, "What's a mother to do?" It is her duty to keep her dependents healthy, and the implication of the ad seems to be that if they do not need breakfast in order to do well at work and school, they may not need the mother at all. With Total as their breakfast, eaten as dependents, they can be better students and workers. The ad upholds mother and home as necessary for the other characters' separate lives elsewhere.

In a dog food commercial, a young husband stops his wife from feeding the dog an inferior product. He knows that dogs need meat and demonstrates to his wife that she has been depriving their dog of the stuff the animal wants and needs. The wife learns her lesson and promises to feed the dog the right product in the future. Note that it is appropriate for the husband to have the secret knowledge that meat is what dogs need, but nourishing remains a mother's task.

A series of ads for a cleanser shows the ease with which a question concerning one woman's competence may be generalized to another, or all, women. Three women are leaving another's home, and two nastily agree that their hostess's home is secretly unclean: "Those pine cleaners must be covering up *something*." In one ad, the hostess overhears; in another, the third guest goes home to her own kitchen and reacts with shock—could others suspect *her* home of having hidden dirt? The drama of competence is made painfully clear, although such familiar elements as children and location in a kitchen may be absent.

The homemaker's role may be precisely specified. She transforms products into food and meals—even cereals are made into "breakfast" or "a balanced diet" for the family—and she employs products that "do the job for her." The job is that of warding off invisible substances, including dirt, germs, decay, and odors.

Other characters have a curious sort of identity. The reason they are present—as child, pet, neighbor, and so on—is immediately apparent. They are not fully under the homemaker's control, but the successful completion of the drama of competence neutralizes whatever identity, knowledge, or competence they have outside the relationship. Thus, children are thwarted in their role as carriers of dirt; the finicky personality of a cat who won't eat is overcome; and neighbors are successfully brought into the home and entertained. The world outside home exists only as a problem for the homemaker as nourisher and cleaner as in the Total ad in which the mother's gift of breakfast makes possible all the outside activities of her family.

One reason for isolating the drama of competence is that it appears to exist in abbreviated or implied form in other ads, as when an older woman tells a young homemaker of her difficulties before discovering some cleansing secret. It would be tempting to understand the drama of competence as simply the American way of representing cakes and cleansers, but this does not explain its presence in one of a series of ads for Sears paints. The announcer explains that in the early days in America gracious living was to be found, and women such as George Washington's mother had to be ready to serve a fine meal. While the camera shows the interior of an old house, the announcer speaks of a cake recipe of Mrs. Washington's and intimates that the cake was served to Lafayette and other such dignitaries who had, we presume, discerning palates. Finally, we learn that we have been viewing her house, which is a historic site, and that its interior is *now* painted with the superior Sears product. Mrs. Washington's secret of competence was invoked only to lead into the topic of the ad and to argue that there is some relevant connection between historic houses and the homes of everyday folk.

These illustrations show that concepts of home and homemaking are closely bound up with the advertising scenario. The categories reappear in situation comedies, although they are differently constrained. We are concerned, in dealing with both ads and situation comedies, with general features around which particular episodes or developments are organized. Since the shows are far more intricate than the ads, I must skim briefly over a highly complex topic at this point.

One of the most apparent differences in comedy homes is the relative flexibility of settings. The advertising drama of competence is typically staged in a kitchen. On the other hand, action in a situation comedy most often occurs in the living room, where we may find Dad's chair or other signs that it is not Mom's domain. In some comedies, the living and cooking areas are not separate rooms, in contrast to all the ads examined.

In the comedies, problems recurrently arise for the homemaker, but they are usually in connection with the interests of other characters, on whom attention is focused. Children appear as distinct personalities with their own problems, not just as carriers of dirt. Pets rarely appear because they cannot be treated as more than dependents. (Such animals as Lassie are, of course, a good deal more than dependents, but their magical qualities may fit in poorly with the versimilitude of the situation comedy home.) Outsiders take on identities as complex as those of family members, as with Mrs. DiLorenzo, the feminist in "All in the Family" or the hero's coworkers in "The Dick Van Dyke Show."

The homemaker takes a smaller, but still important role in the comedies. Often the concept of a show is that the characters can maintain a home without a woman homemaker only with great effort. "Bachelor Father," "My Three Sons," "Family Affair," and "Sanford and Son" deal repeatedly with the problems that aries when no woman is available as homemaker and mother. Their continuity and popularity stands as an argument that the woman homemaker is replaceable, although all others in the home must labor and love intensely to do without her.

There are also shows that deal with the problem of a woman being jobholder and homemaker concurrently. The argument here parallels that of the above mentioned shows: with love, a family does not need a full-time homemaker. Even with a full complement of parents and children, problems do arise, problems that are often phrased in terms of ethics. Accordingly, the shows contain lengthy disquisitions on right and wrong behavior, and all family members contribute their particular bit. "Father Knows Best" brings the scenario into full bloom. Conflicts arise within characters' minds and experience, bringing about discussion in the home; Father knows best; he can probe into difficulties that the children face and he can also act independently outside the home. But Mother has the last word.

In "Good Times," the father and children are consistently tempted to abandon what they all know to be the path of righteousness. Their erring ways—whether in search of money, fame, an exciting boyfriend or the cause of black nationalism—provide most of the plot development. Within a half hour the characters are brought back into line, admitting that the way of life that Florida, the wife and mother, has upheld through the show is the right way. She stands for love, religion, and respect for law, but she does not articulate her stance as a viewpoint. Instead, others present intricate arguments in favor of temptation, detailing all its advantages, until certain home virtues, made explicit only by way of contrast, win out.

All these shows take as an underlying problematic a tension between the maintenance of home as the center of loving relationships, from which people gain strength to act in the world, and the outside world, in which some characters take their place as independent entities. While some situation comedy homes are deviant from the WASP "Father Knows Best" standard (e.g., lacking a mother, ethnic), any home situation is seen as involving enough difficulties to provide plot material for a comedy. While the adds discussed previously focused on the homemaker's ability to do the jobs assigned, the comedies stress the problem of being both a family member and an individual elsewhere: a worker, pal, student, or keen teen. Instead of a drama of competence we find a drama of loyalties. Difficult decisions about action elsewhere are faced in the domestic context; home is the locus of a practical, sensible, just, and loving morality, even on "All in the Family," where practical and just viewpoints are expressed separately, to the detriment of both.

In order to achieve the drama of loyalties, the home is established as both the field of action and as an option. The household emerges as an object of loyalty as well as the scene of shifting loyalties. This is achieved by equating mother and home. The mother becomes a summarizing symbol (Ortner, 1973) whose presence conjures up the entire complex of love, food, security and morality. In contrast to other characters the mother summarizes and elaborates on what is proper and what is not.

The mother's arena of action and her loyalties are overwhelmingly in the home: Maude, the would-be feminist, gives up her hopes of a job so that her husband can count on her being at home, can do well in his store, certain that all is well and his dinner will be on the table on time at home. Maude's yearning for independence is translated into a style of homemaking. She is portrayed in the show as a "real estate person," a label which, after a single episode, implies no commitment or activity outside the home.

The mother, it seems, is constrained to summarize. This is most notable when we compare the role of Florida, first as the maid on "Maude" and then as mother and homemaker in her own "Good Times." As a maid, she is the most articulate character, exposing quite clearly the pretensions of all around her; but as a mother she can only protest vaguely against immorality. The character who inspired "Good Times," then, is muzzled by her role in it. As a homemaker, she must choose between respect for the individuality of her dependents and the general task of homemaking. Her problems now depend on the fact that others mediate between home and the outside.

Although much more remains to be said, it should be clear that common assumptions about settings, actions, and personnel are to be found in situation comedies. The contrast between these assumptions and those of the ads emerges under four headings:

1. The mother and homemaker is central to both, yet in the comedies she is the center around which others act and express themselves. In the ads, she may restrain their self-expression, if it threatens the home, or act so that their contribution is, in the end, only to praise her homemaking.

2. Persons have individuated biographies, interests, skills, and other characteristics in the comedies and, as a consequence, problems of ethical action and conflicts of loyalties inevitably arise. In the ads, however, persons pose problems of homemaking, which can be solved simply through the use of certain products.

3. The comedy home and family are opposed explicitly to other zones—work, school, and the like—which have their own personnel, activities, and, most importantly, special, specific claims on family members. In the ads, such zones lack definition, and actors from different zones are equivalent in precipitating and witnessing the same situation—the homemaker's drama of competence.

4. The difference between acceptable outcomes in the two forms is striking. In the ads, a specific technical problem is solved. As a consequence, dependents may hug homemakers, or guests may admire the clean home, yet these are not the confirmation that the task has been accomplished. Rather, they are the *result* of its successful accomplishment. In the situation comedies, the tasks may be far more diffuse—"being honest," for instance—but whatever their specificity, people's reactions *confirm* successful performance. The characters may show shared knowledge of homemaking and related standards, but the proof of correct action lies in manifestations of love, not in a well-baked cake. One implication of this is that the ads may suggest that a cereal will solve most of a homemaker's problems and worries for all time, that is, they assume that all problems in the home have satisfactory technical solutions. Comedy resolutions, however, are provisional. The momentarily happy comedy home will be upset by a new problem next week and the characters will muster their individual resources to contain it.

These contrasts are not random. The two dramas may be seen as alternate solutions to a single, familiar contradiction in American culture. The contradiction lies in the fact that, for Americans, people are seen as both unique individuals and also in terms of the roles they play. Archie Bunker is both himself and, like many others, a father and worker. Obviously, roles and associated activities cannot be delimited if they depend on satisfying unique individuals with unique motives and needs. To put the matter bluntly, the ads stress that problems of role performance can be overcome or neutralized as a result of proper technique; the comedies assert that individuals, acting in their own unique ways, may accomplish adequate performance despite their deviation from general standards. We may note this both in the posing and the resolution of dramatic problems. Thus, Maude does not say, "What's a mother to do?" when her daughter has no time for breakfast, but instead yells, "Do you have to rub it in . . . the pretty young career girl goes off to work, leaving the tired housewife behind!" A moment later, Maude meets or surpasses housewifely standards in feeding her husband. It is quite clear that she is engaging in parody and wants to point out that she too is an individual. Later, her husband gives in to her, saying, "You gotta do your own thing and do it well to be happy." She kisses him; they agree that the matter over which they have quarreled is behind them, and Maude, with a knowledge granted to no advertising homemaker, says that it is "behind them, ahead of them, to the left, to the right. . . ." Her choice is correct because it is hers but it can be only a temporary solution.

This view of the dramas accounts for the variety of comedy families. In a drama of individuals, where love can affirm individual action as proper in a particular home, the individuals involved need not be all genealogically related, or a family may be precariously maintained without a mother. In contrast, the advertisements do not show sons-in-law, butlers, or others as residents of homes. The ads involve fulfillment of our expectations for the jobs of mothers, fathers, and children and hence show no marginal members in residence. Let me stress that both dramas depend on expectations for the proper activities of status holders. In the ads those expectations are met; in the comedies, individual action is deemed equivalent, in a particular home, to ideal role performance.

The preceding comments do not account for the constraints visible on situation comedy mothers. The problem may be posed a bit more clearly. Female homemakers are confined, in effect, to symbolizing the particularity of their homes. They set the scene in which individual acts are confirmed by love, and they do not move outside it. American notions of sexuality, however, do not explain why Edith Bunker is so vapid, why Maude cannot keep her job, and why other homemakers are more a backdrop than performers in comedies. Articulate and active women do exist in the comedies, but they are never homemakers.

We may note that while the advertising homemaker is the focal actor, constraining others to status positions by serving them, the comedy homemaker is the focal nonactor, around whom all others display their individuality. Neither drama is purely one of individuality or status; the contrast between female homemakers and all others in both dramas summarizes the presence of the contradiction and the possibility of its resolution.

Notes

I am indebted to Janet Dolgin, Nina Kammerer, David Kemnitzer, Richard Kurin, Susan Montague, and other readers for data, confirmation on the coding of particular episodes, and comments on earlier drafts.

1. Ideally, the selection of data and hence the demarcation of dramatic forms should be based on extensive analysis of the forms appearing on TV, the emissions in which form-marking characteristics are neutralized or otherwise ambiguous, and the possibility, within one emission, for a change of form. This paper lacks such an exhaustive basis, although advertisements other than those discussed were examined in order to demarcate the form under discussion. It should be noted that the analysis may not apply to comedies produced before about 1960. While the analysis might help in understanding "The Honeymooners" or the early "I Love Lucy" shows, it certainly would not have the same force in accounting for plotting and characterizations as it does with regard to later comedies. Further work on the stabilization of what is here termed the "drama of loyalties," clarifying the differences between it and the organization of both its predecessors and such nonfamily shows as "The Mary Tyler Moore Show" could well illumine how Americans perceive the family.

References

Ortner, Sherry, 1973, "On Key Symbols." *American Anthropologist* 75, no. 5, pp. 1338-1346.
Schneider, David M., 1968, *American Kinship*. Englewood Cliffs, N.J.: Prentice-Hall.

By training I am a specialist in language and social life in India. I have always believed that studying another society allows an anthropologist to look at his or her own in new and insightful ways. After I completed a research project on the language of South Indian family relationships, I decided to act on this belief and study American family life in television "soap operas." I was well acquainted wth soap operas: I had sensed in myself (with suitable horror) a predisposition to addiction. This fascinated me, as did the knowledge that I could become one of the millions of devoted viewers watching virtually the same few stories repeated again and again year after year. As an anthropologist and student of family life I wanted to understand why these stories were so compelling. The answer I found is contained in "Soap Operas: Sagas of American Kinship."

SOAP OPERAS
Sagas of American Kinship
SUSAN S. BEAN

Each weekday, more than 18 million people (Edmonson and Rounds, 1974:184) tune in their television sets to watch a genre of drama known popularly as soap opera. Soap operas are known to most Americans by reputation, if not through direct exposure, as serial melodramas about doctors and adultery, shown on television during the day, and watched mostly by housewives. In New York City a viewer may select among fourteen half-hour shows aired between 11:30 in the morning and 5:00 in the evening.[1] The large number of soap operas produced and the large number of viewers they attract indicate the significant place they occupy in American life. This paper presents an anlysis of the content of soap operas, which focuses on their major subject, one that is of central interest both to Americans and to anthropologists: the American family.

The story lines of the fourteen soaps available in New York are repeated over and over. The numerous plots and subplots on the program "Days of Our Lives" (summer 1974), for example, are quite typical of soap operas in general. On "Days of Our Lives" (NBC) Bill and Laura are in love, but Laura is married to Mickey; Bob has divorced Phyllis to marry Julie, but Julie really loves another; Susan is married to Greg but his brother Eric is in love with her (will Susan fall in love with him?); Addie is married to Doug, but he and her daughter Julie used to be lovers (are they still really in love?). The triangle involving ties of love and marriage with various complications is the most frequently occurring plot. Each of the fourteen soap operas features at least one triangle, some as many as five.

Plots centered on conflicts between natural and social parentage are also common soap opera fare. Of these fourteen serials, only two programs have none (and one of these did in the recent past); some have as many as three. For example, on "Days of Our Lives," Laura's child is the natural child of Bill, but she is married to Mickey, who thinks the child is his and raises it as his own. The real father of Susan's child is Eric, but she is married to Greg, who is raising the child as his own. The natural father of Julie's child is long dead, and Julie's husband, who has raised the child as his own, is recently dead. Julie feels that she should remarry because a son needs a father.

The people who get into these predicaments are very respectable Americans. The women, if married, are usually housewives. Some work as doctors, secretaries, nurses, and lawyers, but their professional activities remain well in the background. Women doctors, for example, are seldom seen practicing medicine. When a crucial operation is to be performed the doctor is male; female doctors may be shown observing from the operating room gallery. Occasionally, however, a woman's job occurs in the foreground of the drama, usually when it comes into competition with husband, home, and family. The men on the soap operas are doctors, lawyers, and businessmen with a representation of journalist, restaurateurs, and an occasional police officer, architect, or writer. No major, middle-aged, male character is a gas station attendant, a plumber, or a factory worker. Most are professionals, well-educated, and self-employed.

These people represent the achievement of the American dream: financial success, education, independence. They have "made it." (Although, of course, some occasionally falter, businesses collapse, failures lead to drink and so on.) They live in suburban America, in small cities and towns. Much of the action in soap operas take place in the homes of these successful, well-established Americans. The kitchens are large and modern, the furnishing attractive and neat, and the inhabitants fashionably well dressed. The prestigious occupations of the characters, and the middle- to upper-middle-class respectability of their homes is the backdrop against which the action takes place. The problems on which soap opera plots are based lie elsewhere.

Given the sameness of setting and plot, it would appear that the 18 million viewers are willing to watch the same thing over and over again each afternoon. Why? The repetition is certainly not an accident nor the result of poor program planning. Television programming is notoriously ratings oriented. Sponsors want viewers to see their commercials and buy their products, and programs are dropped if their ratings fall too low. In the case of soap operas, the attention to ratings is, if anything, even greater because of the direct participation of many of the sponsors who actually own and produce the programs. If the commercial sponsor participates in the production of the show, and if the sponsor's primary motivation is selling soap, it is obvious that he will provide in his programs what the ratings show the viewers are most interested in watching—the more viewers, the more potential customers. Given the number of viewers, something about the soap operas must be of tremendous interest. Rather than accident or poor planning accounting for the sameness in setting and substance, we have, on the contrary, successful formulas tried and true.

Soap operas are created and produced for American women: 70 to 80 percent of the viewers are women (Edmonson and Rounds, 1974: 184). Most are housewives, but many are working women. American women are (or are supposed to be) homemakers, even if they also hold jobs. One of the major duties of homemakers besides cooking and cleaning is the maintenance and management of family life. Women, as homemakers, take the greater responsibility in raising children, and in maintaining family ties. They remember birthdays and anniversaries with greeting cards, plan weddings, and arrange family dinners at Christmas and Thanksgiving. In America, women are the custodians of kinship.

The most common plots of soap operas, the triangles and problems of parentage, are about establishing and maintaining the family in America. If, in fact, this subject is one that vitally concerns the viewers (American women), it seems likely that the dramas are popular because they deal meaningfully with an area of great interest to American women, the family.[2] In the following pages the picture of the American family contained in the soap operas will be presented. The data on which the analysis is based were gathered from viewing and from monthly plot summaries available in *The Soap Opera Newsletter*.

THE TRIANGLE

On "Days of Our Lives," there are currently five triangles. One of them is the story of Bob, Phyllis and Julie.

> Bob and Phyllis were happily married for many years but now Bob has fallen in love with Julie. Bob decides he must leave Phyllis for he no longer loves her. Phyllis becomes distraught; she thinks about killing Julie. Bob proposes marriage to Julie and she eventually accepts, even though she does not love him, for he can provide her with social and financial security. Can their marriage be successful if Julie does not love Bob (and in fact is in love with another)?

The story begins with a perfect couple who are married and in love. But then something goes wrong. It is in this way that soap operas communicate with their audience about family life—by creating situations that violate the ideal order of the family, then, slowly, over several months working toward the restoration of the ideal.

What goes wrong in this case is that Bob becomes attracted to Julie and begins to lose interest in his wife. After a time it becomes clear to him (and to the audience) that he loves Julie, not Phyllis. There is no explanation for his changing affections. There is some talk about the changes that men go through in middle life, but that does not account for it. Bob himself does not understand why he has ceased to love Phyllis and come to love Julie. He even regrets that it has happened, but it has, and there is nothing he or anyone else can do about the situation. Here we are shown the mysterious nature of love. Love happens all by itself—it comes and goes without reason. People do not have control over it—it happens to them. Thus, even an ideal marriage in which the partners have the best intentions is not permanent or stable, for one of them may fall out of love with the other.

As Bob falls in love with Julie, he falls out of love with Phyllis. In soap operas there is no possibility of being in love with two people at the same time. It may be unclear for a while which appearance of affection is real, which one is love, but it will eventually become clear. The story tells us more about the nature of love: real love can be felt only for one person at a time.

Phyllis reacts violently to the loss of Bob's love and the dissolution of their marriage: she becomes irrational. She believes that Julie is evil and has taken Bob from her. She even begins to think about killing Julie. We are shown that it is insane to believe love can be controlled by acts of will, or that Julie could take Bob's love from Phyllis, or that Phyllis could get it back by killing Julie. Rational, sane human beings know it is no one's fault, and there is nothing anyone can do about it.

Bob, who is now in love with Julie, proposes marriage to her. It is quite natural, in fact inevitable, to want to marry a person one is in love with. (After all, love and marriage go together like a horse and carriage.) Julie decides to marry Bob even though she doesn't love him, because he offers her security The chances of such a marriage being successful are slim, because, we are told, as marriage is the natural outcome of love, a marriage cannot be successful unless built on love. Julie's marriage to Bob will work only if, mysteriously, she falls in love with him. The audience is prepared for problems between Julie and Bob.

The story of Bob and Julie and Phyllis is about love and marriage. It demonstrates that love is a mysterious force beyond our control, an emotion that can be felt only for one person at a time, the natural basis for marriage. Marriage, unlike love, is within our control. We can choose to marry and to divorce, but we cannot choose to love.

Another triangle from "Search for Tomorrow" (CBS):

> Eunice and Doug, a lawyer, are happily married and have a baby girl to whom they are devoted. Eunice decides she would like to fill her spare time, and takes a job as a writer on a local magazine. Her boss, John, is also a lawyer, in fact, Doug's chief rival. Doug disapproves of Eunice's working because it takes her away from their family. After a time he becomes convinced that Eunice is having an affair with John, a belief that has no foundation in fact. He refuses to believe that Eunice is innocent and that she loves only him. Doug asks for a divorce, but Eunice still hopes for a reconciliation. In her misery, Eunice is drawn to John, who offers her advice and consolation. In fact, John is in love with Eunice. The final blow comes when, because of the malicious meddling of outsiders, Doug is crippled in an accident which paralyzes him from the waist down. The love Eunice shows for him is now interpreted by Doug as pity. He refuses to have anything to do with her and the divorce is finalized. John, who is still very much in love with Eunice, urges her to marry him. She is tempted to accept because any future with Doug now seems hopeless. Eunice marries John but does she really love him or is she still in love with Doug?

Again we begin with a situation that appears to be ideal: a loving couple devoted to their baby girl. (It should be noted that there is another long story of how Doug and Eunice achieved their ideal but short-lived bliss.) Doug comes to believe that Eunice is having an affair with John. Doug's suspicions are unfounded. Here we learn that the ideal relationship between a man and a woman includes sex as well as love and marriage. Because they are married, Eunice's sexual involvement should be with Doug alone, because to have it otherwise is a violation of the marriage. It is adultery, but worse than that, it is a symptom that love is felt for another. Sexual involvement is the natural expression of love, just as marriage is the culmination of love. Sex is a sign of love.

From this triangle we also learn something about the nature of love. Doug's belief that his wife was involved with another man led to the ruin of their marriage. The result was as bad as if she really had been involved with another man. Love is something to be exchanged. Just as it can be destroyed when one ceases to give love, it may also be destroyed when one ceases to accept love. The latter, however, is much more unusual, perhaps even evidence of an unbalanced mind. Normal people need love so much they are often tempted, though it is somewhat unethical, to accept love from one to whom they cannot give it (as Eunice is tempted to do with John). As usual, it is easier, if not better, to receive than to give. But Doug is unable to accept Eunice's love, and so he asks for a divorce. He is now saying that, more than being unwilling to accept love from Eunice, he is also unwilling to give love to her, in spite of the fact that there is evidence that he feels love for her. Eunice, who has a normal need for love, is drawn to John, who offers her comfort, friendship, and love. Love, then, is something to be exchanged, to be mutually given and received between a man and a woman.

Doug's subsequent paralysis tells us something more about the relationship between sex and love since he becomes paralyzed from the waist down. Until then he has been only an emotional cripple, unable to give love to his wife even though he loves her. Now, unable to be sexually involved with her, he believes that because he is "less than a man" she can feel only pity and sympathy for him, not love. He has confused the sign (sex) with that which it is a sign of (love). Just as he believed that Eunice was sexually involved with John and therefore no longer loved him, now he believes that since he cannot have sex with Eunice, she can no longer love him. Doug is an emotional and physical cripple. Eunice, who is quite healthy, is drawn closer to John by her need for love.

From the story of Doug and Eunice and John, we learn about the nature of love as something to be exchanged, given and received. A refusal to give or receive destroys the relationship. Because it is easier to receive than to give, what usually goes wrong is that one ceases to give love. Doug is unusual, perhaps abnormal, in being unable to accept love. We also learn about sex. Sex is a sign of love; it is the natural expression of the love between a man and a woman. But it is only a sign and should not be taken for the real thing, as Doug mistakenly does. The connection is a powerful one, but not necessary. Sexual involvement should be restricted to the married couple, who should be in love with each other.

Triangles demonstrate the ingredients, and the connections between the ingredients in the ideal relationship between a man and a woman: the co-occurrence of love, marriage, and sex. Love is the basic ingredient on which the ideal relationship is built. Marriage (which temporally should come second) is the desired cultural culmination of love; sex is its natural expression. Love can only really be felt for one person at a time. Therefore, sex (love's sign), and, of course, marriage (its culmination) should be engaged in only with one person at a time. Sex and marriage are matters of choice, but one cannot choose to love or not to love.

A triangle is a violation of the ideal. The three ingredients do not coincide, but are placed in conflict by being bestowed on different individuals. Thus, Bob is married to Phyllis, but in love with Julie. Eunice is married to Doug, but Doug thinks she is having an affair with John. When the ideal order is lost, the power of love to entail both sex and marriage causes events to move toward the recreation of the ideal order in a new relationship. But the basic dilemma is built in. While the ideal is the everlasting coincidence of love, marriage, and sex, it is in the nature of love to come and go mysteriously; and love is powerful (it conquers all). This is why the triangle is eternal.

PROBLEMS OF PARENTAGE

The second most frequent problem plaguing soap opera characters concerns their relationships with their children. Consider the story of Steven, Alice, Rachel, and Jamie on "Another World" (NBC):

Steven and Alice are married. They are blissfully happy for a while. They would like to have a family but Alice is unable to have children. Steven decides to be more of a father to his natural son, Jamie, with whom, until this time, he has had little contact. He arranges to contribute to Jamie's support and to spend time with him. Rachel, Jamie's mother, is delighted, seeing this as an opportunity to get closer to Steven through their child. Alice is jealous of Steven's relationship with his natural son. Rachel arranges for Alice to discover her alone with Steven in suspicious circumstances. Alice, sure that Steven is involved with Rachel, becomes distraught and disappears with no explanation. Rachel succeeds in her plot. After a time Steven decides to marry her, mainly so that he can be a real father to his son. Eventually Alice returns. Steven and Alice realize they still love each other. With great resistance from

Rachel, Steven manages to get a divorce. Steven and Alice remarry. Disputes over the custody of Jamie begin. Jamie is torn between his love for his mother and his love for his father.

Steven and Alice are happily married. But there is a serious flaw in their happiness. Alice cannot have children. Alice's feeling of inadequacy and her consequent insecurity in her relationship with Steven indicate something about the nature of marriage. Marriage is more than the culmination of the love between a man and a woman (as the triangles have shown). It is the basis on which families are built. Put more strongly, its purpose is to create families. A married couple alone is incomplete.

Indeed, Alice has more to worry about than her inability to produce a family, for Steven has the ingredients for a real family that does not include her. He has a natural son, Jamie. And there is Rachel, Jamie's mother, who would be more than happy to have him.

We are shown by the juxtaposition of these two imperfect situations how things should be. Steven and Alice are in love and married, but cannot have children. Rachel's love for Steven is not reciprocated, and they are not married, but they have a child. The ideal, then, is a man and woman in love and married with a child who is the product of their sexual union. This is a family.

Both Alice and Rachel see in Steven's closeness to Jamie a potential for closeness to Rachel, Jamie's mother. Alice fears it; Rachel feeds it. They believe that the shared creation of a child whom they both love will bring the parents together and make them love each other. The triangles revealed that the ways of love are mysterious and beyond our control. However, the bonds between the parents based on their mutual love for a child, who is tied by blood to each of them, seem to be strong enough to be mistaken for love (Alice), or transformable into love (Rachel), or substitutable for love (Steven). Rachel attempts to capitalize on these beliefs, and she is successful for a time. Alice is convinced that Steven is having an affair with Rachel, and Steven eventually decides to try to make a realy family with Rachel and their son by marrying her. But it cannot work, for although Rachel and Steven eventually decides to try to make a real family with Rachel and Rachel and the arrangement is doomed to failure. Failure is realized when Alice returns and she and Steven reaffirm their love. Rachel has lost Steven to Alice. We have been shown that the basic ingredient of the family is love between a man and a woman. Without that a family cannot successfully be built.

The problem now is what to do about Jamie. Who will get custody? That the problem arises at all tells us several things about the ideal family. This problem emerges only when Jamie's parents split up, indicating that their relationship to Jamie should be as a unit and not as individuals. They should share in his upbringing. The relationship should be between parents and child, not between mother and child, on the other hand, and, father and child, on the other. Jamie's reaction to his parents' separation makes this explicit. For a time he will not speak with his father, because he thinks his father is mistreating his mother. At one point he runs away. Later there is a reconciliation with his father. Jamie's distress is acute. Parents are supposed to be together, a unit. But Jamie's parents are separated and he must relate to them individually but he does not know how.

That custody for Jamie is disputed by his parents indicates something else about the relationship between parent and child. Both Steven and Rachel wish to have legal custody of Jamie because they both love him and want the right to raise him. They base their dispute on the fact that they are equally Jamie's parents. They are both his natural parents, having contributed equally to his conception. Their divorce precludes raising him together as ideally they should; they must compete for him. The ties of blood and love are held separately. The right to raise their son, recognized in legal custody, is different from the ties of blood and love. This is something that parents should hold as a unit. It is clearly undesirable, although possible, for them to have separate social/legal rights and duties with regard to their son.

We learn more about the family from the story of Steve, Carolee, and Eric from "The Doctors" (NBC):

> Steve and Carolee are happily married, and have a daughter of their own, and Steve's son, Eric, from a previous marriage. Eric and his mother were in a plane crash. He was rescued, but she was declared missing and presumed dead. Eric is about 8 years old now and has grown up thinking Carolee is his real mother. Carolee and Steve have decided that she should adopt Eric and become his legal mother. Just as they are about to let Eric know that they have done so, Eric tells them how glad he is that he has a real mommy and daddy and wasn't adopted like one of his friends. With some trepidation, somewhat later, Steve and Carolee tell Eric that Carolee is his adoptive mother, not his natural mother. He seems to take it well, but then one day when Carolee scolds him, he complains that she loves Stephanie, his half sister, more than she loves him. Soon after he runs away.

Eric, whose natural mother is presumed dead, is living with his father and his father's wife, Carolee. Carolee loves him and treats him as her own, but she is not his legal or natural mother. Through the power of the courts she acquires the legal right to raise him, but, of course, she cannot become his natural mother. This is a fact of biology that cannot be changed. Through the juxtaposition of these different kinds of parent-child relations, three aspects of the relationship between parent and child emerge: being a parent (a biological fact), acting like a parent ("raising" a child, a right and duty usually sanctioned by law), and feeling like a parent (love).

Eric had thought that both of his parents, Steve and Carolee, were his natural (biological) as well as his loving and nurturing father and mother. He lets it be known that parents who legally raise and love a child but are not biologically related (i.e., adoptive parents) are not real parents. Through Eric's reaction a relationship among the three ingredients of parenthood is established. The natural connection is presented as basic; the ties of love and nurturing are secondary.

Further, Eric, now knowing that Carolee is not his natural mother, concludes that Carolee loves his half sister (her natural child) more than she loves him. From this we learn something more about the relationship among the three ingredients of parenthood. Parental love is derivative and its sources are known (unlike romantic love, the source of which is mysterious). There are two sources: the biological connection between natural parent and child, and the care given by the parent. Eric's reaction indicates that the first source of love is more powerful than the second. Finally, Eric's attempt to run away is testimony to the importance of the biological connection between parent and child and the profound disturbance caused when it is discovered that the relationship is not what it should be, because, although there are social and loving ties between both parents and their child, the natural bond is defective because it exists with only one parent.

There is an interesting contrast here between the parent-child and man-woman relationships. In the relationship between man and woman, the ideal of a couple united by love, marriage, and sex may be destroyed and recreated over and over. The ideal relationship between parent and child, however, rests on a blood tie which, of course, cannot be recreated. If the blood tie is not present, the relationship between parent and child must rest on love derived from the social tie. Eric believes that this is second best. What he must (and presumably will) learn is that a relationship built on love derived from nuturing is just as good as one built on a blood tie. That is, love as the basis of the parent-child relationship is a substitute for the real thing (blood), but it is a very good substitute.

These two stories tell us about the way relationships between parents and children should be. There are three ingredients that should be present: a blood tie, a social tie, and a bond of love. The blood tie is basic. The love of a parent for his or her child is not as mysterious as romantic love. Its sources are two: the blood tie, and the nurturant relationship between parent and child. The context in which the parent-child relationship should occur is the family. The purpose of marriage is to create families, the integrity of which is ultimately based on the love between husband and wife. Here a connection between triangles and parent-child problems is established. The latter are derived from triangles where sex, marriage, and love are not exclusively held between husband and wife. As in the triangles, these out-of-order relationships between parents and children, and the efforts of the characters to restore order, show us how things should be in the American family.

THE AMERICAN FAMILY

According to the soap operas, then, the American family is built on two sets of relationships: one between husband and wife, and the second between parents and child. Both of these relationships ought to be dyadic. This is obviously so in the case of husband and wife, but also true in the case of parents and child: mother and father should function as a unit in relation to their child. Problems result when relationships that ought to be dyadic become triadic. That is, when the husband or wife becomes involved with another (a triangle), or when the parents do not relate to their child as a unit, but separately as mother and father.

Each dyadic relationship should contain three basic ingredients. A man and a woman should be united by love, marriage, and sex. Parents and child should be united by blood, love, and nurturing. Love is an element in both relationships, but the love between parent and child is different from the love between husband and wife. The former is parental or familial love derived from the blood tie between parent and child, and the nurturing of a child by its parent. It has a beginning but no end. To stop loving your child would be unnatural in the worst sense of the word. The love between husband and wife is romantic love, the source of which is mysterious so that it may begin and may end suddenly. It just happens to people (one falls, not jumps). The two kinds of love are sharply differentiated and people who share familial love are prohibited from sharing romantic love by the incest taboo.

Just as there are two kinds of love, so there are two kinds of biological relationship. The biological connection between parent and child is based on birth and blood, and once it is established it is permanent. The biological connection between husband and wife is sexual union, which is transitory. One may choose (except in the case of rape) whether or not to be sexually involved with another person.

Similarly, there are two kinds of social bond, one between parent and child, and one between husband and wife. Marriage and custody are the legal recognition of social relationships between husband and wife, and parent and child, respectively. Both of these can be initiated or dissolved by participants in the relationship with the approval of society, represented by the courts.

The relationship among the elements of the husband-wife dyad may be contrasted with those of the parent-child dyad. Both are based on natural phenomena, in one case emotional (romantic love), in the other biological (blood). Both have natural expressions, one in sex as an expression or sign of romantic love, the other in parental love as the expression of the blood tie. Just as romantic love may be temporary, so may sexual involvement. Just as a blood tie is permanent, so is its expression in parental love. Only what is natural (but not all of what is natural) can be enduring, and so the social relationships may be given or taken away by society (marriage, divorce, awarding custody).[3]

THE BEGINNING IS THE END

So far we have looked at the family as a static phenomenon. But it has an ongoing aspect too, which is also dealt with in the soap operas. New families are created by the personnel of old families. The old must, in part at least, be destroyed or transformed by the new. There are proper ways to accomplish this: some things ought to be given up, some must be maintained.

The most interesting soap opera plots are concerned with this problem. They are the most interesting because they are the furthest removed from the empirical realities of social life, and most clearly demonstrate that soap operas operate not with the acualities of family life, but with the principles on which it is based. Most often these plots occur as complications of the ones discussed so far. There are at least three varieties of plot that deal with the ongoing aspect of family life: brother-sister incest (a rare but fascinating problem), the triangle involving blood relatives (e.g., mother and daughter involved with the same man, or brothers involved with the same woman), and the mother-in-law. I will comment only on the last of these.

Three versions of the mother-in-law problem are offered. Version one, from "The Doctors" (NBC):

Steve Aldrich is a young successful doctor from an upper-class Boston family. He and his wife Carolee are happily married. Steve's mother, Mona, has been traveling in Europe for several years, leading a carefree, sophisticated life. Suddenly she wires Steve to expect her for a visit. Steve and his mother were very close during his childhood, but as peers. She never liked the role of mother very much. Steve has always called her by her first name. He is delighted that she will visit. Some months pass and it becomes evident first to the audience and then to Carolee that Mona is doing everything she can to break up their marriage. First she tries throwing Steve together with a childhood sweetheart also from a fine Boston family. Then she tries to lure Steve back to an upper-class Boston practice so that he will see for himself that Carolee is not the sort of girl for him. She hopes he will give up Carolee, and stay in Boston with her. Her plot does not succeed. Steve stays with Carolee and Mona goes to Boston alone.

Version two from "Love of Live" (CBS):

> Dan is a young successful doctor from a well-to-do family in Boston. After a stormy courtship he marries Kate, a nice girl from a working class background. But Kate has problems: she was raped by a former lover and is pregnant. Dan's mother, Mrs. Phillips, arrives on the scene, and tries to find a way to break up the marriage. She believes that the baby Kate will have is not Dan's and tries to convince him to get a divorce. When she learns the baby is Dan's she becomes involved in seamy schemes with Kate's ex-lover to keep the information from Kate and Dan. But Dan, even though he believes Kate's baby is not his, goes to Kate and declares his love for her and the child and asks her to let him come back.

Version three from "Search for Tomorrow" (CBS):

> Len is a young successful doctor. Len's mother, a businesswoman, after having lived in Paris for many years, returns home. Len calls her by her first name, Andrea. She is a lonely possessive woman. Len is married to Patti. Because Patti cannot have children, she and Len arrange to adopt a child. Unknown to Patti, Len and Andrea arrange to adopt a baby boy, who is Len's natural son. Andrea, wrongly, thinks that Patti is an incompetent mother and is endangering her grandchild, who is not even Patti's real child. She becomes involved in unsavory plots with a psychotic woman, who is jealous of Patti, to destroy Len and Patti's marriage. She wants Len to divorce Patti and get custody of her grandson, his natural son. She plans to move in with Len and help him raise the child. The outcome of many additional complications is that Andrea's scheme is unsuccessful. Len realizes that Patti is a good mother after all. Patti and Len and the baby move away, leaving a sadder, but wiser Andrea behind.

All of these stories concern the relationships between a mother, her son, and her daughter-in-law. The son, a young doctor, is married to a nice girl. The young doctor's mother arrives on the scene, alone. Because she's "not good enough for him," the mother does not approve of her son's wife and does everything in her power to destroy the marriage.

In these stories two women are placed in competition with each other for a man—the son and husband. The mother wishes to keep him in her family; the wife wishes to take him to form a new family. The son plays a passive role, remaining unaware of what is going on between his wife and his mother. The wife is a nice, relatively powerless victim; the mother is a powerful meddler, with questionable motives. The audience's sympathies lie with the wife and, in the end, the mother is defeated and the young doctor and his bride are happy (for a month or two at least).

The interesting figure in these plots is the older woman. She enters the scene alone. If she has a husband or other children they remain in the shadows. Mona and Andrea have no husbands, and Mrs. Phillips's husband appears only briefly, attempting to discourage her from interfering with their son's marriage. Len is Andrea's only surviving child; Mrs. Phillips has no other children; and Mona's other child does not appear in the story. These mothers have no one but their sons. Each is so resentful of her son's attachment to his wife that she will try almost anything in order to get him to leave his wife.

Mona and Andrea are worldly women, sophisticated, well traveled, youthful, and fashionable: not the motherly type at all. They regard their sons more as peers than as children. Now that they are older and alone, they wish to have their sons to themselves as friends and companions. Mrs. Phillips, on the other hand, thinks she has the right to dictate her son's choice of a wife. She wants to retain control over her grown son.

We learn something interesting about love from these episodes. The bonds between mother and son include blood, parental love, and nurturing. Dan's mother, Mrs. Phillips, wishes to keep all these ties intact. It is clear that she is in the wrong, and that she must give up custody and control over Dan so that he can form a new family. Mona and Andrea also wish to keep their sons but their approach and proposed solution is different: they are willing to give up mothering. They never liked it much anyway, preferring to lead worldly, sophisticated lives. They wish to transform the bond of parental love into something dangerously close to romantic love, thereby remaining or becoming their sons' chief companion. Familial love and romantic love are supposed to be distinct and mutually exclusive. But Mona and Andrea confuse the two, indicating that in some basic way familial love and romantic love are very much alike.

Dan's mother is unwilling to have things change; Andrea and Mona want change but to a state that is not culturally acceptable. None wishes to give up her son, but they each must. The mother who has given birth to the son cannot in later life have him for a consort or keep him as a child. He must become an adult and he must go elsewhere for a mate. So the soap operas contain a kind of social theory of the function of the incest taboo (not unlike Tylor's, Levi-Strauss's, and White's). The mother must give up her son to another woman.

Thus, unlike the bonds of love, marriage, and sex, which (ideally at least) once established, unite a man and a woman until "death do us part," the bonds that unite parent and child do not remain unchanged. The ties of blood and love remain, but parents must give up nuturing when their children are grown. It is only by letting them go that new families can be formed.

CONCLUSION

The soap operas contain a coherent expression of the principles on which the American family is based. Their immense popularity indicates that the picture they present is at least meaningful, and probably very significant, to a large number of Americans. This analysis has demonstrated how the principles on which family life is based are revealed in dramatic dilemmas that violate the ideal order. Elements that belong together in the same relationship are opposed in different relationships. A man is married to one woman but in love with another; a child's natural mother and its legal and loving mother are different women. Resolution is sought in the restoration of the ideal, where this is possible, by uniting the several elements in a single relationship—the man marries the woman he loves; the child learns to accept his legal and loving mother as if she were his natural mother. The analysis of the most common of these dilemmas, the romantic triangles and problems of parentage, reveal the concepts and relations among them that are central to American ideas about the family: romantic and parental love, sex and marriage, blood and nurturing. The analysis of soap operas, then, provides another approach to the study of American kinship, which uses a previously untapped source of data on American ideas about the family.

Notes

I would like to thank my colleagues Emily M. Ahern and Harold W. Scheffler for their comments on earlier drafts of this paper.

1. In 1974.

2. It is also likely that the middle-class uniformity of soap opera characters and settings is the result of an almost exclusive concern in soap operas with the women's domain. The men's domain, the achievement of socioeconomic success, only rarely occurs as an ingredient in soap opera plots. Rather, its successful achievement occurs as a given, a backdrop against which the drama of the female domain is played.

3. Marriage is easy to get and not too difficult to get rid of; custody is hard to get (unless you come by it naturally), and no one wants (or should want) to give it away.

References

Edmonson, Madeleine and D. Rounds, 1974, *The Soaps*. New York: Stein and Day.

Goodlad, J. S. B., 1971, *The Sociology of Popular Drama*. London: Heinemann Educational Books Ltd.

Laub, Bryna R., ed., 1974, *Daytime Serial Newsletter*. (Post Office Box 6, Mountain View, California 94042).

Warner, W. Lloyd, 1948, "The Radio Day Time Serial: A Symbolic Analysis." *Genetic Psychology Monographs* 37:3-71.

I grew up reading Nancy Drew mysteries and was always curious about why they fascinated me. So I had a personal interest in looking at Nancy Drew. As an adult, I became both an anthropologist and a feminist. In recent years, feminist ideas about women's roles in Western society have had a great deal of impact on anthropology. I have never been convinced of the accuracy of feminist explanations of the cause and nature of the plight of contemporary Western women. My work in the Trobriand Islands led me to suspect that the problem is cultural, and it seemed to me that juvenile literature like Nancy Drew stories, which directly addresses the issue of proper adult social roles, could provide data on twentieth-century changes in American ideas about women. So, by looking at Nancy Drew and her fellow juvenile-literature idols, I could kill two birds with one stone: explore Nancy's fascination and delve into what has happened to Western women.

HOW NANCY GETS HER MAN
An Investigation of Success Models in American Adolescent Pulp Literature
SUSAN P. MONTAGUE

This paper investigates success models in American culture. The data are drawn from adolescent pulp literature, with specific attention paid to Horatio Alger and Nancy Drew stories. Baldly stated, the aim of the paper is to explain why in a society once so attracted to Alger's success model, as evidenced by his sales, Nancy Drew, who violates it, sustains an equally great appeal. That this question initially seems trivial or at best somewhat irrelevant to the serious student of American culture is a sad commentary on our views of popular media. It is only recently that anthropologists are attempting to treat mass media seriously as a data source. In large part this stems from ethnocentrism, from the fact that pulp media are defined by us native Americans as frivolous, not serious stuff, intended for leisure relaxation. Actually it is precisely the fact that mass media *is* aimed at leisure time, and *is* voluntarily bought by its audience that ought to lead us to the realization that it contains information that its buyers find particularly timely and topical. I thus hope that this paper not only explicates a particular historical shift in success ideology in American culture, but in addition that it provides a convincing demonstration of the utility of mass media material as a data base for significant cultural analysis.

The best-known body of didactic success literature is a series of stories written in the second half of the nineteenth century by Horatio Alger, Jr. They were, indeed, so successful that Horatio Alger has become an American synonym for success. The books are "how to" manuals, guides to assist young men to properly program their course through adult life. The plots are uniform: a poor youth sets out to find fame and fortune, the rewards given by society to the successful actor. By following aspirants as they seek success, the reader is educated in their methods. He learns the success formula. Alger's formula is simple: its basic tenets are hard work, self-denial, and altruism. Let us look at each of these in turn.

Alger heroes are enjoined to seek rewards through work. Work means holding a paying job in the world of commerce, or business. The heroes are exhorted to devote their lives to work. Devotion is demonstrated by not only holding a job, but also by devoting off hours to improving work skills. It is not uncommon for an Alger hero to attend night school while working during the day. Ragged Dick goes so far as to take in an impoverished but educated boy and pay his lodging in return for tutoring (Alger, 1972). Alger heroes are always happy to spend time with successful older men, learning of and from their business experiences.

In addition, dedication to work also means a certain type of performance on the job. Alger heroes are diligent at their work. They appear on time, and work overtime if necessary. When they find themselves unoccupied they eagerly seek out new tasks to perform. They make sure that each task is done thoroughly and correctly, admitting their failures and attempting to compensate through increased effort.

Dedication to work involves *self-denial*, the second element in the formula. Work is portrayed as both physically and mentally taxing. It strains the individual's resources and tires him. In short, far from gratifying, work does the opposite: it drains. It is the *result* of the worker's effort that gratifies him, not the effort itself. This means that there is always the temptation of more directly pleasurable activities, which might lead the worker away from his tasks. The model therefore discriminates between legitimate and illegitimate gratification. Legitimate gratification comes after the work is completed, and consists of the actor's satisfaction from a job well done, along with society's recognition of that same fact. Society's recognition consists of fame (good repute) and money. Alger defines fame as the most valuable reward. However, these stories are called "from rags to riches" stories because the plots actually center on the search for wealth. Good reputation may in theory be the most important, but without the accompanying wealth the hero would feel deprived, because it is money that tells him and others that his efforts are truly appreciated. Fame and fortune thus ideally go together, fortune validating fame. However, Alger is aware that money may be had illegitimately, and that actors who legitimately make money may later become evil people, and it is for these reasons that he emphasizes good repute while his heroes actually look for dollars.

Illegitimate gratification means using one's resources in ways that render them unavailable for work. Alger defines the most tempting forms of illegitimate gratification as smoking, drinking, and gambling. Smoking is wasteful of money and injurious to health, but of the three is the least pernicious. Whereas in *Mark, the Match Boy* the secondary hero is persuaded to "leave off smoking—a habit which he had formed in the streets of New York" (1962: 382), in *Digging for Gold* the secondary hero smokes and nothing is made of the fact (1968). Drinking is worse. The heroes do not drink, and excessive drinking is used as one of the signs of the antihero.

Gambling is the worst temptation. It wastes time, money, and can lead to theft to cover financial losses. But these are not the main reasons that gambling is so pernicious. Rather it is that the gambler is opposed to the work ethic: he wants to get something for nothing. Smoking and drinking may injure the actor's work capacity, but indulgence in these activities does not necessarily mean that the actor opposes work. With gambling, however, there can be no question. The man who recognizes the proper relationship between work and money cannot gamble, and conversely, the gambler cannot be a truly dedicated worker. Ragged Dick gambles, but only because he believes that he will never amount to more than a poor bootblack. When he decides that he can better himself and seek success, he overtly repudiates gambling, although he apparently still smokes (1962: 75, 110). In *Digging for Gold* the hero, who has a job in a restaurant, is accused of gambling and is at pains to try to clear himself because if thought guilty he will be fired (1968: 88-105).

Thus far, the element of altruism has not entered into the model. Getting rich and famous hardly seems altruistic. However, altruism is in fact the key component. The success is the actor who devotes his life to helping others. Wealth and fame are the expressions of a grateful society, grateful for his efforts on its behalf. It is crucial that Alger defines work as *labor that benefits society*. The hero deserves success because he dedicates his life to assisting others. He is rewarded both for his accomplishments in this line and for the fact that he is willing to routinely forego self-gratification in order to devote himself to his work. One of the most often heard criticisms of Alger books is that the heroes do not really get rich by working hard, but through dramatically helping wealthy actors in nonbusiness crises. Rescuing the banker's drowning daughter, preventing a train crash, or reuniting a man with his long lost son—these are the kinds of actions that earn lavish reward. But this criticism misses the point. Alger maintains that the actor who thinks of others first will always get ahead because he possesses moral character, and is thus deserving. Opportunity will knock at his door.

Achieving success does not permit any relaxation of altruism. The boy who struggles upward in one book is the wealthy patron of another struggling boy in the next. When offered $1000 reward, the already successful Richard Hunter takes it, saying: "Then I will keep it as a charity fund, and whenever I have an opportunity of helping along a boy who is struggling upward as I once had to struggle, I will do it." His benefactor replies: "A noble resolution, Mr. Hunter! You have found out the best use of money" (1962: 381).

The popularity and pervasiveness of the Horatio Alger model is undeniable. Not only did it sell well in the pulp business, but it is striking that *the* American sport, football, is virtually an enactment of this model, to the extent that Vince Lombardi spent his off seasons lecturing businessmen on how to improve worker attitudes and thereby increase profits.

Thus far my data present no problems. Horatio Alger's success formula is simple in its tenets, and has an internal logical consistency. However, difficulties arise when we look at some other adolescent pulp literature. The difficulties concern the role of women. Alger's model is not aimed at women. Rather, women function as the hero's ultimate reward. This is submerged in the stories in the sense that the heroes are always actively seeking reputation and money; but the reason they do this is so that they may support a family either by taking on support of a widowed mother or marrying the sweetheart of their dreams. Women do not actively figure in the stories because they do not compete in the business world: they do not work. Theirs is the complementary realm of the home, and for them, to work is a hardship. It means either that they are too unattractive to attract a husband, or that through misfortune they have been stranded without one. As Huber puts it:

> A cynic once remarked that "a man is a success if he can make more money than his wife can spend." The rejoinder might be: "Yes, and a woman is a success if she can find such a man." A wife not only took the name of her husband, but also her rate of mobility from him. However, one did not speak of a housewife as a "success." A housewife didn't get promoted. There was no way of measuring her achievement. (1971: 5)

We would expect, considering the Alger stories, that there would be a complementary literature aimed at telling girls how to go about finding and attracting a successful man, and that such literature would be centered on domestic roles. In fact there was and is that type of didactic female oriented adolescent pulp literature, but the best-selling series in the United States for the last 45 years has been the Nancy Drew series, and it does not conform to these expectations.

Nancy Drew is but one of many creations of Edward Stratemeyer. Stratemeyer began his career writing Horatio Alger stories after Alger's death, and came into his own with the Tom Swift series. He wound up as *the* teen pulp writer for Grosset and Dunlap, turning out over 800 books under sixty-five pseudonyms (Prager, 1971: 102). As Laura Lee Hope he wrote *The Bobbsey Twins,* as Franklyn W. Dixon, *The Hardy Boys,* and as Carolyn Keene, *Nancy Drew.* Stratemeyer began writing Nancy Drew stories in 1930. To date, over 30 million Drew books have been sold, while Alger sold only around 17 million (Prager, 1971: 73; Alger, 1962: 7). As adolescents hand them around Nancy Drew books have probably been read by some 60 million

American girls and women in the last 45 years. Why?

An examination of the content of the stories indicates that adolescent girls *too* are interested in success, for that is the basic topic. The books document the adventures and achievements of an extremely talented and capable heroine. What are some of Nancy's accomplishments? Well, to start with, she is an expert on Shakespeare, ancient Greece, Chaucer, obscure pottery marks and manufacture, and Mayan cryptography. And as Prager explains:

> For all her intellectual attainments, Nancy is no bluestocking. She rides and swims in Olympic style . . . on one occasion leaping into a bayou with all her clothes on and doing a rapid 500 yards to the shore. She can fix a balky outboard motor with a bobby pin. With no effort, she climbs a rose trellis to the second floor. Pursuing an escaped crook she puts the police on his trail by drawing a perfect likeness of him for them. When the River Heights Women's Club charity show faces disaster because of the defection of its leading lady, Nancy steps in at a moment's notice and wins general kudos with a creditable ballet, although she is recuperating from a sprained ankle. At 100 yards, she plugs a lynx three times with a Colt .44 revolver. Her delphiniums win first prize at a flower show. She floors "Zany" Shaw, a fullgrown law breaker, with a right to the jaw. She is always a barrel of fun at a party, and she ". . . received a lot of applause for her impersonation of Helena Hawley, a motion-picture star who played parts in old-time westerns." What hero or heroine of modern fiction can top that (1971: 78)?

And indeed, even the most successful Alger hero falls short. But these capabilities are merely the window dressing, the backdrop for Nancy's true success arena, criminal detection. Nancy is an accomplished teenage detective, who routinely solves mysteries that baffle the official experts.

Stratemeyer, like Alger, is overtly didactic. He claims that by observing Nancy anyone can learn to succeed as she does in the area of crime detection. The implicit message is that since Nancy's methods do not vary from activity to activity, one can generalize from the explicit model of how she catches criminals to how to succeed in any undertaking.

How does Nancy solve crimes? First, like Alger heroes, she has prepared herself:

> No doubt all of us have scores of times rubbed elbows with some refugee from justice, or have figured in some unimportant incident which actually was one link in a long chain of mystery and adventure. Few of us,

though, have trained our powers of observation and deduction as Nancy had, although by studying her methods it should not be at all impossible for any intelligent reader to learn them. (1933: 13)

Second, Nancy is completely dedicated to her task. Stratemeyer states:

There was something about a mystery which arroused Nancy's interest and she was never content until it was solved. (1930: 6)

"Where there's a will, there's a way," she quoted whimsically. "That old proverb is doubly true in the Crowly case. If there actually is a second will, I'm going to find it!" (1930: 23)

Nancy pursues the solution despite all costs or discomforts. She spends enough time on pleasurable activities to be acceptably sociable, but she is forever leaving a party early to return to the chase.

Nancy is also altruistic. She works to help people, not for reward. She is always modest about her accomplishments, taking true pleasure from the knowledge that she has been useful to others.

In short, Nancy Drew is essentially an Alger success model hero; she functions in the role and according to the standards that he outlined for men. Instead of standing on the sidelines cheering, she is in the heart of the battle. Instead of staying home, she goes out after criminals. How can this be? Why is it that a society that found the Alger model so compelling also supports Nancy Drew? One obvious possibility is that there was a cultural change and that by 1930 women's roles had been redefined so that women might legitimately function in either or both slots of the Alger model. To investigate this hypothesis let us look at how Stratemeyer presents Nancy, the person, and the other most prominent women in the series.

In the first volume, *The Secret of the Old Clock* (1930), the reader is told that Nancy's mother died when Nancy was 9 years old. At that time Nancy took over the adult woman's traditional domestic role of running the household. This included supervising the servants and planning the menus. To her father's surprise she performed this role with an adult's competency. Recognizing that her unusual talents indicated a high intelligence, he encouraged her to develop her mental skills. And since he had no son, but rather an exceptional daughter, he raised her to follow in his professional footsteps:

From her father she had acquired the habit of thinking things through to their logical conclusion. Frequently Carson Drew had assured her that she went at a thing "like a detective." (1930: 6)

Carson Drew, a widower, showered a great deal of affection upon his daughter; it was his secret boast that he had taught her to think for herself and to think logically. Since he knew that Nancy could be trusted with confidential information, he frequently discussed his interesting cases with her. (1930: 6)

Of course, Nancy had an advantage in being so conversant with the professional secrets of Carson Drew, the celebrated criminal lawyer. (1933: 13)

It is thus the combination of (1) exceptional intelligence and (2) an unusually close paternal relationship or masculine identification that results in Nancy's professional interest and capability. However, this is not consonant with the theme of Stratemeyer's didacticism, for he argues that any *ordinary* girl might succeed like Nancy, and it is clear that she is far from ordinary. By the third or fourth volume he downplays this explanation, and instead establishes Nancy's credentials through favorably contrasting her with two other girls, her chums Bess and George.

Bess Marvin and George Fayne are presented as polar types on a scale of femininity. Bess is overly feminine. Physically she is plump with long, curly hair. She has a predilection for food, frilly dresses, and physical comfort. She does not like dirt, danger, and adventure. George, as her name implies, is a tomboy. She has short hair, is boyish of figure, and tends toward foolhardy daring. She constantly gets into physical difficulty through her rashness; her worst tendency is to fall into mudholes. Nancy stands between the two and strikes the ideal feminine mean. She is physically perfect; not too plump, athletic but not boyish. Like George she likes adventure, but she is not foolhardy. Like Bess she likes feminine frills and comforts, but not to the extent of letting them interfere with her activities. This contrast solves Stratemeyer's problem. Outstanding intelligence is dropped as a qualification, as is excessive masculine identification. Rather, Stratemeyer indicates that it is Bess's and George's extreme type of feminine identity that interfere with their competent performance as detectives. He thus ties *work competency* to what society recognizes as *correct femininity*. However, this is sleight of hand. Correct femininity is actually being defined in terms of what the traditional Alger male looks for in a home-centered, admiring consort. Bess and George are undesirably feminine in that they come close to being unappealing to traditional men: Bess threatens to undermine their masculinity with her over-femininity; George threatens to undermine their masculinity with her own. Nancy is the perfect consort, pretty and practical, the very girl Alger defines as the ideal wife and mother. the domestic complement to the successful male.

Stratemeyer is taking advantage of the fact that the traditional definition of the ideal woman involves two components: physical attributes, expressed in face, figure, and dress; and action orientation, expressed in home management. The two are symbolically tied together. Physical attributes are used as indicators of what sort of wife and mother a woman is apt to be. Stratemeyer's sleight of hand lies in substituting a nondomestic job, criminal detection, for home. By applying the physically expressed attributes that conventionally indicate the desirable wife to performance as a detective, he makes it seem natural and acceptable that the ideal woman and the successful detective should be one and the same.[1]

The fact that Stratemeyer made Nancy a girl who is raised like a boy and had to go to such devious lengths to make her seem both the ideal girl and competent worker indicates that by 1930 it was still not legitimate for women to function in the male slot of Alger's model. And there are other instances in the Nancy Drew stories that support this conclusion. For all her activities outside the home, she retains the traditional feminine home role. She directs the servants, tends the garden, cooks on occasion, and acts as her father's hostess. While her work is outside the home she does not go outside to seek work. Instead it comes to her at home in the person of her father and his clients. And while she works like a professional, she maintains an anateur status by refusing to work for money. Her father supports her, and it is implied that later on Ned, her boyfriend, will do the same.

Nancy's relationship with Ned is also significant. He appears early in the series in the role of an Alger hero. He attends a university, is doing well in his classwork, and is the star quarterback on the football team. He belongs to a prestigious fraternity and is extremely popular with the brothers. When Nancy visits him on campus it is in the traditional Alger girlfriend-consort role: her beauty and other feminine charms make her a high-status prize for Ned, and her presence on his arm as his admirer after he has scored the winning touchdown is visible proof of his success. But Ned is not the only winner in this situation. If Nancy is the visible reward for Ned's achievement, in turn, the fact that he wants her validates her own extreme feminine desirability.

While on campus Ned achieves, Nancy admires. Off campus the situation is reversed since it is Nancy who is out solving the mysteries. To salvage Ned's masculinity, he is given an excuse for his inferior performance as a detective. He cannot solve the crimes because he cannot be physically present. He is either off at school or working as a camp counselor. This means that he actually sees Nancy only on rare occasions for very brief periods of time. The fact that Stratemeyer uses Ned to verify Nancy's femininity, and yet does not present her in a realistic romantic relationship again indicates that Nancy's success role is anomalous.

There is additional direct evidence for this conclusion in Stratemeyer's other male-oriented work. The Hardy Boys series provides a good example, particularly since it was written at the same time

as Nancy Drew. Like Nancy, the Hardy brothers are teenage detectives. And just as she has a boyfriend, they both have girlfriends. But
these girls are not like Nancy. Rather, they are wholly old-fashioned,
domestically oriented girls. While the boys go out and solve mysteries,
they stay home and bake. Their basic function in life is to provide food
for picnics and parties. They never have adventures themselves, but
cheer Frank's and Joe's accomplishments. While again Stratemeyer
does not really develop the interpersonal male-female relationship, the
reason here is not that of anomalous sex roles. Instead, it is because the
series is aimed at 9- to 12-year-old boys, who are assumed to reject any
mushy love stuff.[2]

Thus there exists a real cultural contradiction. It really is the case
that American culture has simultaneously contained a success model
defining different, complementary male and female roles, along with a
popular literature in violation of that model. How did this situation
arise?

The desire of women to enter the labor market following upon the
industrial revolution has been thoroughly documented, but as a cultural development it has not been adequately analyzed. Let us jump
ahead and look at the modern feminist argument, again as presented to
adolescents. In *Girls Are Equal Too*, Dale Carson argues that society
should allow and encourage every member to grow and develop as
fully as possible (1973). This she equates with becoming an individual
with a strong self-identity. How does one grow and develop? By pre-
paring oneself for and then working at a career job. Marriage and
housework, she argues, do not provide adequate identity:

> The two saddest results of the double-sex standard are that: one, girls are
> too often kept from useful work and from fulfilling themselves as people
> as well as wives and mothers (1973: 18)

> And believe me, being Mrs. Somebody is not the same as being some-
> body yourself. There's not much sense of personal identity in it and not
> much pride. (1973: 20)

> . . . everybody, not just boys, should be allowed the pride and sense of
> identity that comes with knowing how to earn a living at work one
> chooses to do, at being treated as an adult human being. (1973: 21)

> . . . there is one thing nobody can take care of for someone else. And
> that is, the sense of one's own worth. And what is it worth, in the long
> run, to have the cleanest kitchen floor in the neighborhood? (1973: 67)

Thus the feminist model sees nondomestic, career work as the
basis of all self-identity, not just something appropriate to males. Although in the 1930s Nancy Drew stories the argument is not yet

couched in terms of self-identity, it is clear that the connection between nondomestic, career work and *the* valuable social persona has
been made. And the connection is strong enough to appear in adolescent literature despite the fact that it violates the traditional sex role
ethos seen to lie at the very core of the organization of American
society. Where did this new idea come from that it had the power
to challenge the fundamental postulates of the traditional social
organization?

I would suggest that this idea is a product of the nineteenth-early-
twentieth-century shift away from the religious model of human society to the scientific-physicalist model,[3] and that that shift involved a
partial redefinition of the actor's relationship to his work. Nineteenth-
century pulp literature, including Alger, uses a religiously based
model of human society, wherein man's existence is plagued by his
character flaw, the propensity to sin. Sin equals greed, the desire to act
for one's self at the expense of one's fellow human beings. The ideal
actor is the person who combats this menace by orienting himself
toward the good of others. He possesses moral character insofar as he
exercises self-control to overcome or avoid his own sinful tendencies.
Alger heroes demonstrate their moral character through their dedication to work. The more menial their tasks, the more self-discipline they
manifest by performing them.

However, by the mid-nineteenth century another model of
human society was well developed in academic circles, and was attracting considerable public attention: the scientific-physicalist model.
Malthus, Spenser, and Darwin were among those who argued that the
true laws governing all existence are the physical laws of nature. Far
from being known or knowable through an oracle, God, these laws
remain to be discovered through careful examination of the physical
world. The physicalists did not destroy the model of man's flawed
character. They added to it. Man's existence is plagued not only by
greed, but also by ignorance, and both of these must be combatted if
hunan society is to run properly. The successful actor under either
model is the person who devotes his life to contributing to the fight to
keep society on the right track.

With the shift from God to nature, the quality of what constitutes
significant contribution also shifts, from performing one's duty, however menial, in the face of temptation, to confronting the challenge of
the unknown, and by the creative application of one's mind, rendering
it known. The ideal worker moves from the dedicated altruistic drudge
to the creative thinker. Whereas Alger heroes are rewarded for being
good clerks, miners, and busboys, Stratemeyer's heroes are explorers,
scientists, inventors, and detectives. They are rewarded for their intellectual feats, for their ability to see solutions missed by other actors.

The shift from work as an expression of moral character to work as
an expression of creativity affects women in two ways. First, a new

option is open to men that is denied to women in their home-centered role. Whereas women express only their altruism in their labor, men in addition use their work to express their mental interests and abilities. The housewife is stuck virtuously scrubbing floors while her husband, equally virtuous, has the thrill of inventing penicillin, exploring darkest Africa, of being the first to fly over the South Pole. Being cheated of the fun and adventure of discovery is a prominent feminist theme. It is coupled with the fear of being thought a bore for not having had exciting adventures. Second, and more important, while the scientific-physicalist model does not deny the need for moral character, it removes it from the realm of the problematical so far as men are concerned. This is because as work becomes the vehicle of self-expression, the lure of temptation decreases. Work is no longer drudgery, but is exciting and interesting. The actor no longer needs to be rewarded for disciplining himself to work, because he enjoys working. Stratemeyer's heroes cannot be distracted from their work because it is the most pleasurable pastime they can imagine. It is no longer only the results of working that are rewarding, but doing the work itself. As maintaining proper work orientation ceases to constitute a problem, the possession of moral character ceases to be the distinctive feature of the outstanding actor. The problematical quality shifts to intellectual ability, and it is this that is rewarded by society. Women laboring at home are left struggling to achieve social value in terms of a quality which, for men, has been devalued and superseded by another. So long as both sexes were rated on the performance of their respective roles by the same criterion, moral character, the division of labor did not necessarily mean that the sexes differed in social worth. Being Mrs. Somebody *was* the same as being Somebody one's self, because Mrs. Somebody was worthy of her outstanding husband only insofar as she too had demonstrated her excellent moral character. Turn-of-the-century pulp such as *Poppea of the Post Office* (Wright, 1909) and *Girl of the Limberlost* (Porter, 1909) does not treat women as lacking social value or identity. Instead it deals with the development of the woman's moral character through correct performance of domestic roles, and it looks for the moral woman to match the moral man. But as the work model changed, woman became socially inferior to men, denied by the division of labor the chance to utilize and demonstrate their intellectual capabilities, and struggling instead to attain the devalued attribute of moral character. And we find Nancy Drew trying to straddle the old model of what it means to be a woman and the new model of what it means to be a valuable social actor.

Nancy is transitional between the two models, and it is striking that a transitional figure has lasted so long. However, 45 years after her inception she still outsells all other pulp literature for girls. This is largely because the cultural conflict between the traditional moral ethos and the changed work ethic defies any easy resolution, and continues to pose a real problem for Americans of both sexes. The devaluation of the female role leaves women with two unappealing choices: to sacrifice self-identity, or by moving into the male work arena, to deny their femininity. Men are confronted with the question of how to define masculinity in the face of female intrusions. But it is interesting that Nancy outsells more modern pulp, which presumably would more accurately reflect the state of the question in current society.

Although I have not conducted an exhaustive survey of the adolescent pulp of the 1950s and 1960s, what little I have read does indeed propose a different solution to the problem. Donna Parker may be taken as a typical case. The formula is superficially the same as Nancy Drew: the heroine is a teenage girl detective confronted with a mystery. But there the resemblance ends. In *Mystery at Arawak* (Martin, 1957), Donna has been given a job as a camp counselor. She is concerned about her ability to perform the job adequately, a concern that Nancy never manifests. She is also concerned about her feminine desirability. One of the other counselors is extremely pretty and in heavy demand for dating. Donna envies this girl. Another counselor is extremely smart, but shunned by the boys. Donna sympathizes with her. In the conclusion Donna realizes that the pretty girl feels handicapped by her looks, just as the bright girl feels handicapped by her brains. Donna concludes that she herself is lucky to be adequate looking, but not beautiful, and adequately smart, but not brilliant, and thus socially acceptable.

The solution here involves manipulation of the same symbols used by Stratemeyer. The pretty girl is in a bind because her feminine looks, which make her attractive to men, also signal the traditional feminine domestic orientation. This constitutes a problem now openly recognized by literature: the equation of domesticity and lack of intellectual creativity. Being defined as femininely desirable also means being defined as stupid or at best vacuous. The bright girl suffers the bind in reverse. Just as the feminine girl cannot be smart, the smart girl cannot be feminine. She is left desexed, and effectively ostracized from male-female social relationships.

This literature defines the problem much more clearly than did the earlier, in that it states the issues rather than glossing over them. But unfortunately, direct statement of the issue does not facilitate a satisfactory solution. The tactic that Martin invokes is simple compromise. If it is impossible to be both perfectly feminine and truly creative, perhaps it is possible to be somewhat feminine and somewhat creative. Donna retains enough feminine attributes to attract at least some men, and also enjoys the modicum of creativity that will not actually threaten their masculinity and hence repel them. But the solution is inadequate because Donna winds up in the same bind that constitutes the essence of the problem in the first place: she is second rate. She does not even get to solve the mystery! Martin leaves it to the smart girl to do that. Donna may bridge the gap between being a real woman and being creative, but she cannot close it. Nancy, for all Stratemeyer's sleight of hand, remains the more appealing character precisely because she enjoys the best of both worlds, the preferable solution however much he had to juggle his symbols to attain it.

SUMMARY

This paper documents a partial shift in success models in American culture due to changing definitions of meaningful work. As the definition of meaningful work went from performance of routine tasks to discovery and mastery of the unknown, a chain reaction was set off. Desirable actor qualities shifted, leading to a reassessment of the sexual division of labor. Because the sexual division of labor lay at the core of American social organization, this created a severe conflict, which still plagues us today. Girls' adolescent pulp literature deals with this conflict because its subject matter is women's roles in society. However, it is confronted with a heavy task. To take on the problem squarely is either to deny American social organization by rejecting the definitions on which it is constructed, or to repudiate the moral base around which American society operates by denying the scientific-physicalist model of the universe, which asserts that the valuable social actor equals the creative worker dedicated to conquering the unknown. The pulp literature has been unwilling to do either of these, and instead has attempted various compromise solutions, all of them inadequate because the two postulates really are irreconcilable. As the very recent girls' feminist literature indicates, there is a current move toward a genuine solution through repudiation of the traditional social organization. However, the continued popularity of Nancy Drew literature, which masks the contradiction and essentially wishes it away, is an indication of the magnitude of difficulties that confront so radical an undertaking, and the corresponding reluctance with which Americans approach it.

Notes

I am grateful to Julia Hecht, David Kemnitzer, John Kirkpatrick, Roy Wagner, and Madeline Schwenk for their comments on earlier drafts of this paper.
1. A further indicator of the sleight of hand is that the girls' feminine identities are, in the final accounting, the result of their parentages. Bess and George are first cousins. Their mothers are sisters. Nancy has no mother. Bess

has learned to be over-feminine from her mother, while George is in rebellion against hers. Nancy, the example of perfect femininity, is untouched by motherly influence, and somehow mysteriously achieved her perfection without any adult female role model on whom to pattern herself.

2. Prager offers a more complete summary of the Hardy Boys series in *Rascals at Large.*

3. I am indebted to John Kirkpatrick for the term "physicalist."

References

Alger, Horatio Jr., 1962, *Ragged Dick and Mark, the Match Boy.* New York: Collier.

—1968, *Digging for Gold: A Story of California.* New York: Collier.

Carson, Dale, 1973, *Girls are Equal Too: The Women's Movement for Teen-agers,* New York: Atheneum.

Huber, Richard M., 1971, *The American Idea of Success.* New York: McGraw-Hill.

Keene, Carolyn (Edward Stratemeyer), 1930, *The Secret of the Old Clock.* New York: Grosset & Dunlap.

—1933, *The Sign of the Twisted Candles.* New York: Grosset & Dunlap.

Martin, Marcia, 1957, *Mystery at Arawak.* New York: Whitman.

Porter, Gene Stratton, 1909, *Girl of the Limberlost.* New York: Grosset & Dunlap.

Prager, Arthur, 1971, *Rascals at Large, Or The Clue in the Old Nostalgia.* Garden City, N.Y.: Doubleday & Co., Inc.

Wright, Mabel Osgood, 1909, *Poppea of the Post Office.* New York: Grosset & Dunlap.

As with many other contributors to this volume, Regelson's interest in this topic stems from earlier fieldwork in another culture. His research in India focused on the meaning and significance of food in a society renowned for its dietary restrictions. The author takes up the same theme in this essay and suggests that the bagel is much more than a basic vehicle for Sunday breakfast.

THE BAGEL
Symbol and Ritual
at the Breakfast Table
STANLEY REGELSON

What could be more American than apple pie? And what could be more Irish than corned beef and cabbage, more Italian than pizza, or more Jewish than bagels and lox? Yet, these foods have become "typical" ethnic dishes only in America; in their native lands, they lack equivalent notoriety.

Food, like any other element of material culture, has a variety of implications. However, American anthropologists, reflecting this culture's puritanical attitude toward food and eating, have concentrated on nutritional and ecological considerations while regarding an interest in flavor and symbolism as frivolous. In contrast, this essay follows the examples of Levi-Strauss (1963) and Leach (1964) and adopts a symbolic analysis. Specifically I intend to comment on the remarkable growth of the custom among American Jews of eating lox and cream cheese on a bagel on Sunday morning. The symbolic value of this secular ritual demands attention since it can not be explained in relation to economics, nutrition, or ecology. The practice may in fact be a weekly ritual enactment of an ancient belief by means of which many contemporary American Jews maintain their sense of religious affiliation and identity.

JEWISH FOOD CATEGORIES

Before addressing the bagel ritual itself, it is appropriate to offer some background information on traditional Jewish food categories. This specific topic has been of interest to many scholars because the categories have survived for many centuries over a wide area without substantial change. Also, they are part of an explicit and patterned fabric of permitted and taboo behaviors; and they are regarded as central to their religion by the Jews themselves. The Jewish food laws can be divided into four elements: (1) All animal and vegetable components of food must be derived from approved species; (2) warm-blooded animals must be ritually slaughtered; (3) blood of slaughtered animals must be removed by ritual soaking; and (4) dairy products and meat products may not be mixed. The first two rules are the concern of male ritual experts outside the home, and the last two are household matters, which come under the supervision of women.

Traditional Jewish labels posit the existence of two major food categories: *kosher* ("clean" or "fit") and *treyf* ("impure"). The latter derived from the Hebrew word meaning "torn," probably referring to game or carrion. Kosher foods are further divided into *pareve, milkhik,* and *fleyshik.*

Pareve foods include all *kosher* foods of plant or chemical origin; and of animal origin, honey, eggs, *kosher* insects, and *kosher* fish. These cold-blooded animals are not subject to the ban on blood and rules for slaughter require only that the animal be spared unnecessary pain. *Pareve* foods cannot pollute other foods, and are ritually neutral. If a *milkhik* or *fleyshik* ingredient is added to a *pareve* food, it ceases to be *pareve.*

Milkhik (dairy) foods include all dairy products produced from the milk of *kosher* animals: milk, butter, cream, cheese, whey, as well as their derivatives. Any food that contains a trace of these items is defined as *milkhik.*

Fleyshik (meat) foods are those produced from the meat of *kosher* mammals and birds, which must be slaughtered by a ritual expert and drained of blood. In the home, the housewife then ritually salts and bathes all exposed surfaces of the meat to remove remaining traces of blood. Only then does it cease to be *treyf,* and is fit to be cooked and eaten.

However, it is taboo to mix *kosher milkhik* food with *kosher fleyshik* food. If the two are brought together, the result is *treyf.* Not only is the result unfit for consumption, but the vessel itself is defiled.

> In order to create a "fence around the law" the rabbis ordained that the separation of meat and dairy must be as complete as possible. Thus, separate utensils, dishes, and cutlery must be used for dairy foods and meat. . . . These must be stored separately, and when washed, separate bowls (or preferably sinks) and separate dishcloths (preferably of different colors to avoid confusion), must be used. If meat and milk foods are cooked at the same time on a cooking range or even on an open fire in a closed oven, care should be taken that the dishes do not splash each other and that the pans are covered. (Rabinowicz, 1971: 40)

As a result, the life of an orthodox Jewish housewife resembles that of a nuclear chemist in a radiation laboratory. Foods are polluted, not only if the categories are actually mixed, but if they are consumed or prepared too close in time or space:

> According to the Talmud (Hul. 105a), one may not eat milk after meat in the same meal. However, strict observance demands an interval of as long as six hours between eating meat and dairy dishes. . . . It is permit-

ted to eat meat immediately after milk dishes, provided that the mouth
is first rinsed and some bread eaten. (Rabinowicz, 1971: 40)

The prohibition against mixing dairy and meat is assumed to stem
from the biblical triple injunction against boiling a kid in its mother's
milk (Ex. 23:10, 34:26, Deut. 14:21). However, the reason for the
generalization of this specific prohibition to include all meat and dairy
foods has not been demonstrated. In approaching this problem some
scholars have even argued that the prohibition was one of the original
Ten Commandments (Frazer, 1919). The broader prohibition against
mixing meat and dairy in general is no easier to explain. For example:
"Abraham ibn Ezra maintained that the reason for the prohibition of
[meat with milk] was 'concealed' even from the eyes of the wise"
(Rabinowicz, 1971: 46).

Some Talmudists have associated the rule with the humanitarian
requirement that a parent bird be chased from her nest before the
young are taken (Deut. 22: 6-7). Maimonides felt that "Meat boiled in
milk is undoubtedly gross food, and makes a person feel overfull"
(Rabinowicz, 1971: 43). More recently, Martha Wolfenstein has linked
the rule to "the impulse of the infant to bite and eat the milk-giving
breast" (1955: 436); and Mary Douglas has written that the prohibition
"honors the procreative process" (1971: 78). The literary critic Isaac
Rosenfield (1949) has stated that a reference to sexual behavior is contained in the taboo. He draws attention to the fact that the word *treyf*
applies to forbidden sexual alliance as well as forbidden food. This
suggestion is pursued here and its association with the seemingly far-
removed topic of bagels, lox, and cream cheese will be clarified
shortly.

The rule against exogamy that labels as *treyf* marriages between
Jews and gentiles is well known. Less well known are the menstrual
regulations, set forth in the Bible (Lev. 15:19-14) and practiced until
modern times. These require that a maried woman and her husband
abstain from all physical contact during her menstrual period and for at
least a full week thereafter. At that time, she is expected to go to the
ritual bath (*mikve*), where she is immersed in water that symbolically
removes the pollution associated with menstruation. During these
twelve days, when the word *treyf* is also applied to the woman, she and
her husband are not only barred from sexual relations, but ideally
should not touch or indeed even hand things to each other. Sexual
congress between a man and a menstrous woman (*niddah*) is a mortal
sin, for which death by divine retribution may be expected (Lev. 20:
18). Virgins, unmarried women, and widows are not required to use
the *mikve*, and are therefore always *treyf* (Ganzfried, 1928 IV:20). A
bride must go to the *mikve* before the marriage is consummated; and
the flood of defloration (whether it actually appears or not) is also

considered defiling and requires a visit to the *mikve*. Furthermore, the role of the marriage ceremony in establishing the fitness of sexual relations is made plain. Thus Jews are instructed that: A bride without the wedding blessings is forbidden to her husband like a *niddah* (Kallah 1:1).

As indicated, animals chosen from among the *kosher* species are slaughtered ceremonially by ritual experts. First, I propose that this ritual is perceived as symbolically equivalent to the ritual of marriage with women of Jewish origin. It was also mentioned that after the meat has arrived in the household, it is ritually washed by women, which transforms it into edible food. Second, I suggest that this activity is symbolically equivalent to the *mikve* ritual. The ritual bath is perhaps the only Jewish ceremony taking place outside the home that is supervised by women.

Hence, there is an identification of the female sex with *fleyshik*, which implies a similar relationship of the male to the *milkhik* category. In other words, there is a symbolic correspondence of milk with semen and masculinity in contrast to meat with menstrual blood and femininity.

Consider the following folktale in this light:

> The milkman (or the man selling milk in the dairy) claims that his milk is perfectly kosher . . . because water which he pours into the pail is taken from the "kosher" Mikvah or Ritual Bath. (Schwarzbaum 1968: 368)

The humor is derived from a simultaneous breaking of both food and sex taboos across symbolic levels.

It is ,now possible to appreciate why the coming together of *milkhik* and *fleyshik* results in a substance unfit for human consumption. Two products of the same household representing different categories are not permitted to come into contact. This arrangement strongly resembles a type of rule we are all familiar with, the incest taboo. For a society with powerful symbolic precautions against marriage with outsiders, it is not surprising to find equally strong symbolic precautions against marriage with certain group members.

The original biblical prohibition against boiling a kid in its mother's milk, which seemed only dubiously related to the broader question of *milkhik/fleyshik* categories, can now be interpreted as a symbolic prohibition against the mixing of closely related members of opposite sex. "You shall not boil a kid in its mother's milk" (Deut. 14:21) emerges as the equivalent of "You shall not bring shame on your father by intercourse with your mother" (Lev. 18:6). The reason for the aforementioned triple biblical repetition of this injunction, and for the ultimate expansion of this narrow prohibition into a veritable maze of dietary rules, is now less puzzling. The set of dietary rules cited earlier is now recognizable as isomorphic (i. e., structurally equivalent) to a set of marriage rules: (1) marriage with an "outsider" is forbidden; (2) sexual relations are permitted only after a consecrated marriage; (3) sexual relations are permitted only during the period following the ritual bath; (4) marriage within the prohibited degrees of kinship is prohibited.

The relationship between food and other cultural categories should now be somewhat more recognizable, so that it is possible to approach the specific problem of lox and cream cheese from a similar perspective.

THE BAGEL RITUAL

The bagel (beygl), derived from the German *Baugel* (little bracelet), is a doughnut-shaped roll made from high-gluten flour. Simmered in boiling water for two minutes before baking, it has a unique chewy texture. Lox is smoked salmon, prepared so that it is bright red and has the texture of raw fish. There are two kinds: ordinary lox and Nova Scotia. The former is considerably saltier than the latter, but the difference between the two is not meaningful to the custom. Lox is an anglicized spelling of the German Yiddish words for salmon (*Lachs, laks*). Cream cheese is the same high butterfat soft cheese generally available in the United States.

The bagel itself is only one of a number of traditional Jewish smallbreads. Among the others are kaiser rolls, salt stengels, and bialystokers, which have faced into obscurity as the bagel has grown more popular. Because of their odd recipe, bagels are produced by specialized bakers in bagel factories, but never at home. Bagel factories, traditionally located in cellars, are numerous wherever there is a concentrated Jewish population. Jews living far from such centers now make provision for the shipment of frozen bagels, since the chemical additive that keeps bread fresh cannot be added to bagels without destroying the characteristic texture.

Lox is only one of a wide variety of smoked and pickled fish preparations that the Jews brought with them from northeastern Europe. Herring, the fish formerly most often linked with Jewish culture, is the subject of innumerable Jewish jokes, usually on the theme of fish as "brain food." Unlike herring, a food of the poor, lox has always been a costly luxury.

Cream cheese, a western European product, is not a part of the material culture that the east European Jews brought with them to America. However, farmer cheese and pot cheese were traditional to this immigrant group. The substitution of cream cheese for pot cheese in traditional Jewish recipes has resulted in another felicitous development, cream cheese cake.

In questioning older Jews, both immigrant and American born, about the traditional Sunday morning combination of lox with cream cheese on bagels, they often become uneasy. They answer, "Bagels and cream cheese, yes. Lox and bagels, of course. Bagels on Sunday morning, why not?" However, what they are uneasy about is the realization that the wide distribution of the custom that we are discussing is primarily a post-World War II American phenomenon. In fact, there is nothing traditional or European about this specific food combination or its ritualized consumption. The explosion of its popularity among American Jews is a contemporary cultural development.

The suggestion that flavor accounts for the popularity of the combination is not very helpful. Although this is the reason most often expressed by informants, the rationale is undermined by the fact that quite different flavors may be produced depending on the type of lox used. Consequently, the explanation must lie elsewhere.

In recent years, the term "bagels-and-lox Judaism" has become a favorite theme of rabbinical sermons in the United States. It is used to refer pejoratively to those Jews who avoid the synagogue and neglect traditional religious practices, yet adhere strongly to "frivolous" secular customs. Concretely, this translates into the fact that there are many Jews who will never voluntarily enter a synagogue, but manage to perform the bagel ritual every week. Despite the self-consciously secular nature of this ritual, it is possible to show a direct relation to traditional Jewish religious symbolism involving the principle of *havdalah* ("distinction"), which is a basic element of Jewish cosmology.

The prime reference of the word *havdalah* is the distinction between the Sabbath and the week, the name of the weekly ceremony performed at the close of the Sabbath, intended to "draw a clear line" between the sacred and profane portions of the week. The *havdalah* prayer reads in part:

> Blessed are Thou . . . who makest a distinction between holy and profane, between light and darkness, between Israel and other nations, between the seventh day and the six working days. Blessed art Thou, O Lord, who makest a distinction between holy and profane. (*Services* . . . 1928: 433)

Other "distinctions" include the preveiously mentioned dichotomies between *kosher* and *treyf*, heaven and earth, eternity and time, male and female. Eternity in this instance refers to the "end of time" or "end of days," the period following the coming of the Messiah ,and the raising of the dead. The set also includes the distinction between the upper and lower parts of the human body: "If no garment or girdle separates the upper part of his body from the lower [a man] is not allowed to utter anything holy" (Ganzfried, 1928 1:12).

In this regard the navel (*pupik*) is traditionally seen as the midpoint of the body, connecting the upper part with the lower. As such, it is an important landmark of Jewish folk anatomy, so that the word *pupik* occurs frequently in jokes and metaphors. For instance, a recent television special on Yiddish culture repeatedly jump-cut in shots of a navel, with the label "PUPIK" as an easy laugh-getter.

The following joke illustrates the navel's folk anatomical function:

> A man was born with a gold screw in his navel. Considering it a disfigurement, he traveled all over the world inquiring how to remove it, to no avail. Finally a rabbi told him, "You should accept the fate you were born to. But if you cannot, go home and go to sleep. You will dream that there is a golden screwdriver under your pillow. Use it to unscrew your navel. When you wake up, the screw will be gone." Everything happened as the rabbi had said. On waking, the man walked to the window, took a deep breath . . . and his behind fell off.

The navel connects the sacred and profane parts of a human being in two dimensions—one natural and one supernatural. First, it marks the juncture of the upper part of the body with its mental (godlike) functions and lower part with its physical animal functions. Second, the navel marks the link between the invisible soul and the visible body. At the moment of birth, each human being is marked with a navel, which spirtually binds body and soul into a single unit. The Jewish mother often worries lest her newborn infant cry too energetically. "He might rupture his *pupik*," that is, the link between spirit and flesh might be sundered.

The world is conceived as having a structure similar to the human body, with the holy city Jerusalem perceived as the navel. Thus, to the ancient Jews and later to medieval mapmakers, Jerusalem was located at the physical center of the world. Furthermore, it is believed that the earth and heaven are actually connected at the site of the temple in Jerusalem, making it the place most suitable for prayer.

> Associated with [the] description of the temple and Jerusalem is the idea that the place is also the center of the world and the *tabbur ha-avez* ["the navel of the earth"]. . . .
>
> As the navel is set in the middle of a person, so is Erez Israel located in the center of the world, Jerusalem in the center of Erez Israel, the Temple in the center of Jerusalem, the *heikhal* ["altar"] in the center of the Temple, the ark in the center of the *heikhal*, and in front of the *heikhal* is the *even shetivyah* ["foundation stone"] from which the world was started. (*Encyclopedia Judaica Jerusalem,* 1971 9:1557-1558)

Thus, it was believed that this foundation stone was the physical spot at which eternity is joined to time. Furthermore, "According to one view, Adam was created from . . . . the site of the Temple" (*Encyclopedia Judaica Jerusalem,* 1971 9:1557). This conception of Adam (who, having a navel, must have been umbilically linked directly to the Creator) repeats and unifies the same references (cf. Eliade, 1959).

Therefore, as the *havdalah* ceremony mediates between the Sabbath and the new week, the navel mediates between soul and body, and the Temple mediates between heaven and earth.

Furthermore, in Jewish culture, bread of any kind signifies man's material needs and is specifically seen as the symbol of earth itself. The prayer over bread refers to it as being brought forth from the earth, and also contains a reference to the first man, since the word for earth (*adamah*) contains Adam's name. Similar to a simplified folkview of the human body, or like the map of the world mentioned above, the shape of the bagel symbolically represents a navel mediating between the earthly and the divine. It is not surprising, therefore, that the first written reference to the bagel was in "the Community Regulations of Cracow, Poland, for the year 1610, which stated that bagels would be given to any woman in childbirth" (Rosten, 1968: 26).

THE END OF TIME

A basic teaching of Judaism is that at the end of time, in the days of the Messiah, the distinction between the material and the spiritual, the profane and the sacred, will cease to exist. In fact, the cessation may be seen as a precondition to the coming of the Messiah, as in the following tale:

> A rabbi returns home and finds his wife in bed with a peasant. In reply to his reprimand, she says: "Rabbi, you have told me that the Messiah will come only at one of two moments—when all men are good, or when all men are bad. I know the time can never come when all men are good, so I am doing my share to bring about the second alternative."

This joke expresses the underlying logic of Shabbatism and Frankism, heretical movements of seventeenth- and eighteenth-century Judaism, which declared that the "End of Days" had come. This heresy, *antinomianism,* also avowed that the serious sins of Judaism were actually meritorious. This inversion of standard morality was based on the Talmudic assumption that with the coming of the Messiah the commandments would be abolished and fasts converted into feasts (Scholem, 1971). "Indeed, some say that all the animals that are unclean in this world will be declared clean by the Holy One in time to come" (Midrash Tehillim 164:4).

At the beginning of time, we are told, God created the distinctions that made a primal chaos "without form and void" (Gen. 1:1) into light and darkness, heaven and earth, sea and dry land. Undermining these distinctions prematurely would restore the world to chaos. But at the end of time, signaled by the coming of the Messiah, the obliteration of the opposed domains will mark the coming of a higher order. In two contemporary Jewish ceremonies performed weekly in the home, the dissolution of these dichotomies is symbolized. On Friday evening the Sabbath is welcomed by the lighting of two candles; on Saturday night the new week is ushered in with a braided candle containing two wicks. Among the contrasts that would be neutralized at the end of time is that between the living and the dead since the dead would be raised in their corporeal bodies.

Hence, in the days of the Messiah, the Law that governs the temporal world will cease to hold; its burden on Israel will be lifted. The division between profane and sacred, dead and living, body and spirit, red meat and white milk, female and male, will no longer apply. Prohibitions pertaining to these divisions will also no longer be meaningful. Consequently, Shabbatai Zevi, proclaimed by his followers in the seventeenth century as the Messiah, pronounced a benediction on "Him who permits the forbidden" (Scholem, 1971: 1223), and he "abolished" the fast of Tishah be-Av and turned it into a feast. A successor to this Messiah also preached: "a complete reversal of values, symbolized by the change of the 36 prohibitions of the Torah . . . into positive commands. This included all the prohibited sexual unions and incest" (Scholem, 1971: 1246).

LOX AND CREAM CHEESE

From the perspective of this analysis lox differs from all other preserved fish preparations in one way: it is as red as blood. The glossy redness of the fish, in combination with the opaque whiteness of the cheese, results in a striking contrast. Indeed, children frequently refuse to eat lox because of its visual resemblance to raw meat. The coming together of these two foods produces a visual pun. Although a permitted combination, lox and cream cheese give the appearance of violating the strong taboo on mixing *milkhik* and *fleyshik*.

This suggestion can be supported from another direction since in many other cultures the ritual use of white and red refers to male and female, respectively. The reference to semen and menstrual blood, often perceived as the two elements required for conception in folk biology, lies just beneath the surface of this symbolic opposition. Indeed, this idea is made almost explicit in the Talmud. "The white substance . . . is supplied by the man, from whom come the child's brain, bones, and sinews; the red substance . . . is supplied by the woman, from whom comes its skin, flesh, and blood" (Niddah 31a).

The persistence of the categories red and white are apparent in association with meats and wines in our culture. Interestingly enough salmon is the only fish eaten with or prepared in red wine. However, these associations go well beyond the kitchen and dining room. The folk tradition that links the (red) rose with females and sexual passion and the (white) lily with males and divine passion is a case in point. The television commercial for a popular wine producer that involves a leering male suggesting a "little white" for him and a "little red" for his female companion and finally a "little rose" for both of them later suggests the ability to communicate effectively at this symbolic level.

However, to return to our primary interest, it can be appreciated how through the use of salmon, a color-marked fish with a fleshlike texture, an obvious reference to meat is being made. In this case, the combination of lox and cream cheese, through a series of intermediate metaphors, can be seen as a reference not only to the breaking of the surface taboo against mixing meat and milk, but a violation of the incest taboo itself. We have often been told, by Freud and Levi-Strauss, among others, that the incest prohibition is a denial of the individual's needs in favor of those of the group, and thus the very foundation stone of human society. Also relevant is the fact that incest was among the practices of antinomian heretics. Thus the consumption of lox and cream cheese is ritual reenactment of an anticipated event—the elimination of the distinctions that govern social behavior of this world after the coming of the Messiah.

The last question is, why should this symbolic reversal be enacted on a Sunday morning, which is normally associated with the Christian, not the Jewish, Sabbath? This paradox can be resolved by bearing in mind that in Judaism the weekly cycle ends with the Sabbath on the seventh day, the day the Almighty rested after creating the universe. Leach (1961) calls attention to the reversals often marking calendric rituals that involve a reversal of a cycle before it resumes. In the case of the Jews, we have repeated examples of this phenomenon. For example, on the weekly Sabbath the Jews, who have a strong mercantile tradition, are prohibited from handling money (Ex. 23:12). At Yom Kippur during the first days of the New Year, the most important ceremony is one at which all vows made in the previous year are declared void. Further, traditionally during the Sabbatical year, farmers were forbidden to sow their crops (Lev. 25:1-7). Following seven sabbatical cycles, every fiftieth year was a year of Jubilee. Ideally at this time slaves were restored to freedom and land restored to its original owner (Lev. 25:10). Finally, the coming of the Messiah was to result in the great overturning of all rules.

Few American Jews strictly observe the Sabbath, and the Sabbatical year and the Jubilee are almost unknown today as religious concepts. However, Sunday morning is the time of the first light after the close of the Sabbath. It is both a symbol and repetition of the moment when time began, the moment when the Creator proclaimed, "Let there be light" (Gen. 1:3). As such, it is the point at which any new era must begin. Similarly, the trumpet (*shofar*), which announces the Jewish New Year, is blown not at the initial evening service but the following morning. Admittedly, few Jews who perform the Sunday bagel ritual observe all the dietary laws. Yet those who do eat bagels, lox, and cream cheese feel that in some way they are affirming their Jewishness. I submit that by symbolically breaking the incest rule at a fixed time representing the moment of Creation, these Jews are confirming their adherence to the fundamental structure of a Messianic faith.

Therefore, this meal results in the coming together of symbolically significant substances defined by certain specifically Jewish values at a time of declining interest in traditional ritual, and the abandoment of the strongest strictures upon food, sex, and marriage. In short, it is an unconscious expression of religiosity and ethnic identity.

Most of the practitioners of this ritual will be startled at the analysis presented here, and deny its validity. Yet we should be aware that anthropologists often encounter and are not surprised by unconscious representations of this type in other cultures. However, we expect that literates such as ourselves are more rational and that ideology will be close to the surface. Yet, we have evidence here that literacy is no bar to such representations or submerged symbolic statements. Indeed, it is in our own society that we may have the opportunity to study the way in which such symbolic representations come into existence.

References

Doublas, Mary, 1971, "Deciphering a Meal." In Clifford Geertz, ed., *Myth, Symbol, and Culture*. New York: Norton.

Eliade, Mircea, 1959, *The Sacred and the Profane*. New York: Harper & Row.

Encyclopedia Judaica Jerusalem, 1971, New York: Macmillan.

Frazer, James, 1919, *Folk-Lore in the Old Testament*. London: Macmillan.

Ganzfried, Solomon, 1928, *Code of Jewish Law*. (Kitzur Shulchan Aruch) New York: The Star Hebrew Book Co.

Leach, Edmund, 1961, "Two Essays Concerning the Symbolic Representation of Time." In Edmund Leach, *Rethinking Anthropology*. New York: Humanities.

—1961, "Animal Categories and Verbal Abuse." In Eric H. Lenneberg, ed., *New Directions in the Study of Language*. Cambridge: MIT Press.

Levi-Strauss, Claude, 1963, *Structural Anthropology*. New York: Basic Books.

Rabinowicz, H., 1971, "Modern Views of the Dietary Laws." *Encyclopedia Judaica Jerusalem*, 6:26-46.

Rosenfeld, Isaac, 1949, "Adam and Eve on Delancey Street." *Commentary* 8:385-387.

Rosten, Leo, 1968, *The Joys of Yiddish*. New York: McGraw-Hill.

Scholem, Gerson, 1971, "Shabbatai Zevi." *Encyclopedia Judaica Jerusalem,* 14:1219-1254.

Schwarzbaum, Haim, 1968, *Studies in Jewish and World Folklore.* Berlin: De Gruyter.

Services for the Day of Atonement, 1928, New York: Hebrew Publishing Co.

Wolfenstein, Martha, 1955, "Two Types of Jewish Mothers." In Margaret Mead and Martha Wolfenstein, eds. *Childhood in Contemporary Cultures.* Chicago: University of Chicago Press.

COFFEE
The Bottomless Cup
LAWRENCE TAYLOR

INTRODUCTION

As these essays illustrate, the anthropologist's prerogative is to wonder about both the bizarre and the obvious. The bizarre is typically of little interest to anyone else, while to most the obvious does not call for explanation. However, the anthropologist as outsider often finds that it is precisely those practices which the members of a particular culture consider most practical and reasonable that strike him as most odd. Perhaps the ultimate fate of the anthropologist is to become a professional outsider and thus a stranger even to his own culture. In this estranged state he is liable to be suddenly amazed by those things he had once been happy enough to take for granted.

In this condition I was struck one morning with wonder at my personal, and my culture's, preoccupation with coffee. I must have been particularly outside myself, for there are few elements of American culture in which I am more avidly involved that those associated with coffee. More than an avid consumer, I am also a believer in everything I am supposed to about what coffee does for me as a social being.

What particularly caught my attention was the waitress's smiling acquiescence to my silent demand for a second cup. I merely looked up, and through the medium of silent language, she knew and responded. However, what impressed me on that occasion was not that she knew I wanted more coffee, but rather that, in the market place of the restaurant, the second and subsequent cups would be free.

Consequently, later that day, I asked my class for their opinion on the "bottomless cup." The first thing they did was close their notebooks, since they reasoned that the professor was no longer talking about real anthropology. Instead he was catering to an obsession with the obvious. Why the bottomless cup of coffee? Several expert informants in the guise of former waitresses immediately volunteered to disabuse me of any fanciful anthropological explanations. Being good natives they suggested that coffee is free after the first cup for a practical reason. Coffee is made in large amounts and it will get stale if not dispensed quickly. In a similar vein, although cheaper, the labor involved in making a cup of tea might make it ultimately more expensive than coffee, so that refills must be paid for.

Like a good anthropologist, I began the investigation of a cultural phenomenon by questioning the natives. Their responses were re-corded as evidence of their "system of thought," but also discounted as inadequate since all the answers were too utilitarian. Americans in particular like to think of themselves as a practical people; thus practical explanations must be immediately suspect.

Is it not possible, I queried, that the production of restaurant coffee by the vatful, as opposed to the one-cup-at-a-time tea, was the result of coffee usages, rather than the other way around? In England, I pointed out, the situation is the reverse. There, tea is made by the pot and can be had in quantity at no extra charge, while if available, coffee is typically instant and prepared by the cup. It is unlikely that the English are unaware of the possibility of mass-producing coffee, or of the convenience of tea bags. They evidently had chosen to make tea the sort of drink that coffee is to us. But what *is* coffee to us?

SYMBOLIC IMPLICATIONS

A helpful student observed that ". . . You invite someone 'over for coffee'." Everyone recognized that the phrase had symbolic as well as literal implications. In America, if someone moves into a new neighborhood and they are not shortly thereafter asked "over for coffee," they would become anxious. Certainly this is not because they are unable to brew a pot for themselves. Consequently, coffee offering has to be examined in the same fashion as any repetitive and significant behavior in an exotic culture.

As anthropologists have long recognized, exchanges are the very lifeblood of social relationships. In a particular culture the items and terms of exchange are appropriate to the specific social relationships. The gift is never pure, but rather sets in motion a process of continual giving and receiving. The recipient understands that the offering stands for a whole series of future exchanges in which he is now obliged to involve himself. A Christmas card from the Smiths requires one in return. An invitation to dinner is more than a free meal; in addition it is an obligation to reciprocate. This does not imply that people view such invitations entirely in this light, since more than likely they are happy to enter into these exchange relationships. What thrills them, if thrilled they are by the reception of the Christmas card or dinner invitation, is not that they got something for nothing. Rather, they are delighted at the prospect of a new social relationship which is implied in the gift.

In many cultures a food offering holds a particularly important place in symbolizing the quality of a social relationship. The high caste Brahmin of India is very fussy about who cooks his food for him; not for fear of poison, but of ritual pollution. Moreover, this transmittable impurity has more to do with the preparer's social position than his personal cleanliness. The exchange of particular foods thus becomes such an important aspect of a social relationship as to stand for or symbolize it. New Guinea pig feasts, for example, are often the most important means of affirming the social solidarity of large groups of people. In Ethiopia some people define those families with whom they interact daily as the "people we drink coffee with."

So it is in suburban America, where the invitation "over for coffee" initiates a socially significant system of exchange. The reason an individual becomes disconsolate at not receiving such an overture lies in the social implications of such an invitation. In effect, coffee stands for, or symbolizes, a certain type of social relationship in America which we call neighborship.

Neighborship

The dictionary informs us that the word *neighbor* comes from the Old Teutonic *neagh-gebur,* meaning 'near-hut.' Neighborship therefore was a social relationship based on the proximity of one dwelling to another. The Old Teutons probably had little choice in recognizing such a tie, since in a tiny hamlet there was little chance, or sense, to remaining socially aloof from one's fellow hut-dwellers.

Neighborship is important in every culture, but its form and meaning will vary greatly. Among middle-class Americans it is not surprising that neighbor implies a very different category of person and relation than was true for the Old Teutons. In the suburbs there is a great deal of choice in the formation and maintenancy of neighborship ties. A family is surrounded by row after row of houses from which only a relative few are selected with whom to enter into neighborship. Proximity, however, remains a vital criterion; the essence and cultural justification of the neighborly relation remains the physical nearness of one dwelling to another. Americans feel that the physical nearness of abodes also calls for a degree of social nearness. The social involvement implied in the relation, however, is limited. For example, we still distinguish between friends and neighbors, both in word and in deed. The neighborly relation is initiated with the offer of coffee, which may or may not evolve into friendship. The invitation means, "Come over and begin being my neighbor." In other words, prepare to receive and reciprocate a whole series of possible exchanges, of which coffee is only the first. Others will then follow, such as the classic requests to borrow the lawnmower or cup of sugar.

Although compared to kinship or friendship, neighborship may seem a relatively insignificant social relation in America, it is nevertheless vital to our daily lives. By establishing understood relations of neighborship the suburban family provides itself with casual access to a whole series of goods and services. Moreover, the restrictions Americans put on the closeness of neighborship may add to its usefulness. Many ties of this type can be upheld simultaneously, whereas the maintenance of an equal number of full-fledged friendships might prove socially exhausting.

It may be objected that coffee is used in many more ways than as a ritual exchange of neighborship. While this is true, the anthropologist's concern is with the cultural meaning of a particular symbol, like coffee, and this is not necessarily found in the analysis of the item's use. Experience is not quantitative, so that the ritual function of a substance does more to define its symbolic meaning than a thousand mundane uses.

Perhaps this proposition can be clarified by looking at color categories which also have symbolic meanings in all cultures. For example, blackness is strongly associated with death in American ritual contexts. However, in the course of a year, blackness is experienced in a thousand insignificant forms. Yet blackness still means death when confronted in a ritual context, such as Halloween, when the witch's black cat means "black, like death." In a similar fashion, the use of coffee to initiate neighborship, and its recurring exchange, may do more to define its meaning to us as a cultural symbol than the thousand papercupsful consumed in less meaningful social contexts.

In pursuing the coffee exchange topic in class, another student remarked that "When I was a little girl, when my mother wanted to begin gossiping with her neighbor, she would say, 'Can't you see we're having coffee?' " An anthropologist from Africa would have to assume from that remark that there is some sort of taboo against children observing their parents and other adults consuming the sacred fluid. In reality, though, the child is being asked to leave in code. Remarkably enough, the child understands very early that the meaning is, "Leave, we're about to engage in the privileged exchanges of friendship—children are not eligible." The mother in this instance used the word "coffee" to symbolize the whole range of neighborly exchanges, and the child took her meaning correctly.

What is more, coffee is the typical American non-alcoholic adult beverage. As a rule, children do not drink it, and if they do, adults may show some discomfort and are likely to comment on the oddity. Evidently the coffee-drinking child is suspect; perhaps he is faking a taste for coffee in order to seem grown-up. The "adults only" proscription may even be buttressed by bogus chemistry. One student's mother had warned her that coffee was sexually dangerous for children. Indeed, I can remember not liking coffee as a child but developing a taste for it, along with several other adult pastimes, only a few years later.

Coffee in the neighborship context is not only an adult fluid, but its exchange is between close hut-dwellers. In some communities in suburban America to fully participate in neighborship requires a home of your own, whether it be a split-level colonial or a high ranch. The Irish bachelor of forty without a farm is still a "boy" and the suburban American without a home of his own is not fully adult in the eyes of others. "Come over to my house for a cup of coffee," also means, "I have a house, too." The relationship therefore is one based upon social and economic equality as well as physical proximity.

Evidently coffee is the offering most suited for the exchange between householders. Although other items may be passed back and forth, coffee normally initiates the neighborly relationship. As with a New Guinea pig feast, a periodic repetition of the coffee exchange is felt to be necessary to proper maintenance of the relationship.

The Household Social System

How is it that in America coffee becomes the typical exchange medium in the relation between hut-dweller and hut-dweller? Looking inside the hut helps to answer the question. The ideal model of the household social system is as follows: the husband wins the bread, and the housewife makes the coffee. Which is to say, the husband provides the raw materials and the housewife cooks them for their common consumption. The food exchanges involved are numerous, and coffee is neither the most economically or nutritionally important. However, it plays a rather singular role in the three exchange ceremonies of the average American family day—breakfast, lunch and dinner. Coffee is the opening presentation which begins the domestic day. It also has the balanced opposing function, for after dinner coffee closes the expected meal exchanges.

In the household, as in neighborship, coffee occupies the unique position of symbolizing an entire series of exchanges, and TV commercials, as they so often do in America, make the point clearly. The unfortunate woman who cannot cajole her husband into taking a second cup of coffee has profoundly failed as a homemaker. This analysis does not mean that the commercial is not trying to sell a product, but there is something sensible in the choice of coffee for this sort of message. If she could not make tea, would she be a similar failure? Although such a commercial is unreal since few divorces have followed from poor coffee-making alone, the submerged message is profound. In our culture, coffee stands for the entire range of responsibilities and exchanges involved in homemaking. The inability to make a decent cup of coffee therefore implies total failure.

CONCLUSION

Thus coffee symbolizes, among other things, the household itself. If one family seeks to establish relations with another, what more appropriate invitation than "Come over for coffee"? We distinguish, as has been said, between friends and neighbors. Friendship is a social relation between individuals. You can choose your friends, as the old saw goes, but you can't choose your relatives. Can you choose your neighbors?

Yes, in the sense that it is possible to select a neighborhood. But once this is done, choices are narrowed considerably, since neighborship necessarily involves physical proximity to others. Freedom to enter into the relationship is also restricted by the fact that one family member may draw others into the web of neighborship. In the absentee-husband suburbs, the housewife may more often than not choose the neighbors, and soon after whole households rather than just individuals are involved.

The bearing these cultural associations have on the price of coffee in restaurants is apparent in an examination of the restaurant context. The coffeehouse customer is greeted by a "hostess," and after eating "her food" (since professional cooks are discreetly hidden in the kitchen), she offers the customer more coffee at no extra charge. The food must be paid for, since the relation between the customer and the restaurant is that of two strangers meeting in the marketplace. Yet the restaurant is evidently also trying to be a pseudo-household by giving away coffee to guests. This explains the emphasis on service and the use of such household symbols as the hostess. There is in this an invocation through the imagery of householdness. Even though socially a stranger, the customer must be made to feel, in some sense, like a neighbor, and in American only coffee can create this illusion.

What is more, Americans are willing to believe in these images. The real test of the importance of a cultural role is in the effect of its breaking. The prices on the menu may rise their predictable two percent per month and no one flinches. After all, these are affairs of strangers. But let the coffeehouse suddenly terminate the bottomless cup and the customer is outraged. What is upsetting is not the rising cost but the abrupt conclusion of neighborship.

This restaurant-customer interaction in the peculiar case of coffee is more intelligible in light of the meaning of coffee as an American symbol. Much of that meaning emerged in an examination of the symbolic social characteristics of American neighborship. The special considerations various cultures afford to specific foods are always valuable paths to understanding their social categories. No matter how sophisticated or technologically advanced, no culture perceives food only as nourishment. In other cultures, different food symbols are important, but in America, good coffee makes good neighbors.

Jill Dubisch was first exposed to the health food movement by her mother, an early follower of the teachings of Adelle Davis. Later, as an anthropologist, she was intrigued by the growing popularity of the movement and the impact it had begun to have on American culture. She first approached the topic from the perspective of medical anthropology, as part of cross-cultural studies of diet and nutrition. Such studies suggest that some of the practices of the health food movement, as well as the basic health food dictum that there is indeed a relationship between food and the maintenance of health and prevention of disease, may have a good deal of validity. However, the author came to realize that there is more to health foods than this, and that the approach of medical anthropology alone is not sufficient for understanding the movement. It was necesary to bring in concepts from another of the author's areas of interest — religion and symbolism — in order to account for both the growing popularity of the health food movement and the fact that, for those who become deeply involved in it, it can become a total way of life. This movement thus provides a rich and fascinating area of analysis for an anthropologist, since it both allows and requires the utilization of a variety of anthropological concepts and approaches for its understanding.

YOU ARE WHAT YOU EAT
Religious Aspects of the
Health Food Movement
JILL DUBISCH

Dr. Robbins was thinking how it might be interesting to make a film from Adelle Davis' perennial best seller, **Let's Eat Right to Keep Fit.**
Representing a classic confrontation between good and evil — in this case nutrition versus unhealthy diet — the story had definite box office appeal. The role of the hero, Protein, probably should be filled by Jim Brown, although Burt Reynolds undoubtedly would pull strings to get the part. Sunny Doris Day would be a clear choice to play the heroine, Vitamin C, and Orson Welles, oozing saturated fatty acids from the pits of his flesh, could win an Oscar for his interpretation of the villainous Cholesterol. The film might begin on a stormy night in the central nervous system. . . .

— Tom Robbins, **Even Cowgirls Get the Blues**

I intend to examine a certain way of eating, that which is characteristic of the health food movement, and try to determine what people are communicating when they choose to eat in ways which run counter to the dominant patterns of food consumption in our society. This requires looking at health foods as a system of symbols and the adherence to a health food way of life as being, in part, the expression of belief in a particular world view. Analysis of these symbols and the underlying world view reveals that, as a system of beliefs and practices, the health food movement has some of the characteristics of a religion.

Such an interpretation might at first seem strange since we usually think of religion in terms of a belief in a deity or other supernatural beings. These notions, for the most part, are lacking in the health food movement. However, anthropologists do not always consider such beliefs to be a necessary part of a religion. Clifford Geertz, for example, suggests the following broad definition:

> . . . a *religion* is: 1) a system of symbols which acts to 2) establish powerful, pervasive, and long-lasting moods and motivations in men by

3) formulating conceptions of a general order of existence and 4) clothing these conceptions with such an aura of factuality that 5) the moods and motivations seem uniquely realistic. (Geertz, 1965: 4)

Let us examine the health food movement in the light of Geertz's definition.

HISTORY OF THE HEALTH FOOD MOVEMENT

The concept of "health foods" can be traced back to the 1830s and the Popular Health movement, which combined a reaction against professional medicine and an emphasis on lay knowledge and health care with broader social concerns such as feminism and the class struggle (see Ehrenreich and English, 1979). The Popular Health movement emphasized self-healing and the dissemination of knowledge about the body and health to laymen. One of the early founders of the movement, Sylvester Graham (who gave us the graham cracker), preached that good health was to be found in temperate living. This included abstinence from alcohol, a vegetarian diet, consumption of whole wheat products, and regular exercise. The writings and preachings of these early "hygienists" (as they called themselves) often had moral overtones, depicting physiological and spiritual reform as going hand in hand (Shryock, 1966).

The idea that proper diet can contribute to good health has continued into the twentieth century. The discovery of vitamins provided for many health food people a further "natural" means of healing which could be utilized instead of drugs. Vitamins were promoted as health-giving substances by various writers, including nutritionist Adelle Davis who has been perhaps the most important "guru" of health foods in this century. Davis preached good diet as well as the use of vitamins to restore and maintain health, and her books have become the best sellers of the movement. The titles of her books, *Let's Cook It Right*, *Let's Get Well*, *Let's Have Healthy Children*, give some sense of her approach.) The health food movement took on its present form, however, during the late 1960s when it became part of the "counterculture."

Health foods were "in," and their consumption became part of the general protest against the "establishment" and the "straight" lifestyle. They were associated with other movements centering around social concerns, such as ecology and consumerism (Kandel and Pelto, 1980: 328). In contrast to the Popular Health movement, health food advocates of the sixties saw the establishment as not only the medical profession but also the food industry and the society it represented. Food had become highly processed and laden with colorings, preservatives, and other additives so that purity of food became a new issue.

Chemicals had also become part of the food growing process, and in reaction terms such as "organic" and "natural" became watchwords of the movement. Health food consumption received a further impetus from revelations about the high sugar content of many popular breakfast cereals which Americans had been taught since childhood to think of as a nutritious way to start the day. (Kellogg, an early advocate of the Popular Health movement, would have been mortified, since his cereals were originally designed to be part of a hygienic regimen.)

Although some health food users are member of formal groups (such as the Natural Hygiene Society, which claims direct descent from Sylvester Graham), the movement exists primarily as a set of principles and practices rather than as an organization. For those not part of organized groups, these principles and practices are disseminated, and contact is made with other members of the movement, through several means. The most important of these are health food stores, restaurants, and publications. The two most prominent journals in the movement are *Prevention* and *Let's Live*, begun in 1920 and 1932 respectively (Hongladarom, 1976).

These journals tell people what foods to eat and how to prepare them. They offer advice about the use of vitamins, the importance of exercise, and the danger of pollutants. They also present testimonials from faithful practitioners. Such testimonials take the form of articles that recount how the author overcame a physical problem through a health food approach, or letters from readers who tell how they have cured their ailments by following methods advocated by the journal or suggested by friends in the movement. In this manner, such magazines not only educate, they also articulate a world view and provide evidence and support for it. They have become the "sacred writings" of the movement. They are a way of "reciting the code"—the cosmology and moral injunctions—which anthropologist Anthony F. C. Wallace describes as one of the important categories of religious behavior (1966: 57).

IDEOLOGICAL CONTENT OF THE HEALTH FOOD MOVEMENT

What exactly is the health food system? First, and most obviously, it centers around certain beliefs regarding the relationship of diet to health. Health foods are seen as an "alternative" healing system, one which people turn to out of their dissatisfaction with conventional medicine (see, for example, Hongladarom, 1976). The emphasis is on "wellness" and prevention rather than on illness and curing. Judging from letters and articles found in health food publications, many individuals' initial adherence to the movement is a type of conversion. A specific medical problem, or a general dissatisfaction with the state of their health, leads these converts to an eventual realization of the "truth" as represented by the health food approach, and to a subsequent change in lifestyle to reflect the principles of that approach. "Why This Psychiatrist 'Switched'," published in *Prevention* (September, 1976), carries the following heading: "Dr. H. L. Newbold is a great advocate of better nutrition and a livelier life style. But it took a personal illness to make him see the light." For those who have experienced such conversion, and for others who become convinced by reading about such experiences, health food publications serve an important function by reinforcing the conversion and encouraging a change of lifestyle. For example, an article entitled "How to Convert Your Kitchen for the New Age of Nutrition" (*Prevention*, February, 1975) tells the housewife how to make her kitchen a source of health for her family. The article suggests ways of reorganizing kitchen supplies and reforming cooking by substituting health foods for substances detrimental to health, and also offers ideas on the preparation of nutritious and delicious meals which will convert the family to this new way of eating without "alienating" them. The pamphlet, *The Junk Food Withdrawal Manual* (Kline, 1978), details how an individual can, step by step, quit eating junk foods and adopt more healthful eating habits. Publications also urge the readers to convert others by letting them know how much better health foods are than junk foods. Proselytizing may take the form of giving a "natural" birthday party for one's children and their friends, encouraging schools to substitute fruit and nuts for junk food snacks, and even selling one's own baking.

Undergoing the conversion process means learning and accepting the general features of the health food world view. To begin with, there is great concern, as there is in many religions, with purity, in this case, the purity of food, of water, of air. In fact, there are some striking similarities between keeping a "health food kitchen" and the Jewish practice of keeping kosher. Both make distinctions between proper and improper foods, and both involve excluding certain impure foods (whether unhealthful or nonkosher) from the kitchen and table. In addition, a person concerned with maintaining a high degree of purity in food may engage in similar behavior in either case—reading labels carefully to check for impermissible ingredients and even purchasing food from special establishments to guarantee ritual purity.

In the health food movement, the basis of purity is healthfulness and "naturalness." Some foods are considered to be natural and therefore healthier; this concept applies not only to foods but to other aspects of life as well. It is part of the large idea that people should work in harmony with nature and not against it. In this respect, the health food cosmology sets up an opposition of nature (beneficial) versus culture (destructive), or, in particular, the health food movement against our highly technological society. As products of our industrialized way of life, certain foods are unnatural; they produce illness by working against the body. Consistent with this view is the idea that healing, like

eating, should proceed in harmony with nature. The assumption is that
the body, if allowed to function naturally, will tend to heal itself.
Orthodox medicine, on the other hands, with its drugs and surgery and
its nonholistic approach to health, works against the body. Physicians
are frequently criticized in the literature of the movement for their
narrow approach to medical problems, reliance on drugs and surgery,
lack of knowledge of nutrition, and unwillingness to accept the validity
of the patient's own experience in healing himself. It is believed that
doctors may actually cause further health problems rather than effect-
ing a cure. A short item in *Prevention*, "The Delivery is Normal—But
the Baby Isn't," recounts an incident in which drug-induced labor in
childbirth resulted in a mentally retarded baby. The conclusion is
"nature does a good job—and we should not, without compelling
reasons, try to take over" (*Prevention*, May, 1979: 38).

The healing process is hastened by natural substances, such as
healthful food, and by other "natural" therapeutic measures such as
exercise. Vitamins are also very important to many health food people,
both for maintaining health and for healing. They are seen as components of food which work with the body and are believed to offer a
more natural mode of healing than drugs. Vitamins, often one of the
most prominent products offered in many health food stores, provide
the greatest source of profit (Hongladarom, 1976).

A basic assumption of the movement is that certain foods are good
for you while others are not. The practitioner of a health food way of
life must learn to distinguish between two kinds of food: those which
promote well-being ("health foods") and those which are believed to be
detrimental to health ("junk foods"). The former are the only kind of
food a person should consume, while the latter are the antithesis of all
that food should be and must be avoided. The qualities of these foods
may be described by two anthropological concepts, *mana* and *taboo*.
Mana is a type of beneficial or valuable power which can pass to individuals from sacred objects through touch (or, in the case of health
foods, by ingestion). Taboo, on the other hand, refers to power that is
dangerous; objects which are taboo can injure those who touch them
(Wallace, 1966: 60-61). Not all foods fall clearly into one category or the
other. However, those foods which are seen as having health-giving
qualities, which contain *mana*, symbolize life, while *taboo* foods symbolize death. ("Junk food is . . . dead. . . . Dead food produces
death," proclaims one health food manual [Kline, 1978: 2-4]) Much of
the space in health food publications is devoted to telling the reader
why to consume certain foods and avoid others. ("Frozen, Creamed
Spinach: Nutritional Disaster," *Prevention*, May, 1979. "Let's Sprout
Some Seeds," *Better Nutrition*, September, 1979.)

Those foods in the health food category which are deemed to
possess an especially high level of *mana* have come to symbolize the
movement as a whole. Foods such as honey, wheat germ, yogurt, and

sprouts are seen as representative of the general way of life which health food adherents advocate, and Kandel and Pelto found that certain health food followers attribute mystical powers to the foods they consume. Raw food eaters speak of the "life energy" in uncooked foods. Sprout eaters speak of their food's "growth force" (1980: 336).

Qualties such as color and texture are also important in determining health foods and may acquire symbolic value. "Wholeness" and "whole grain" have come to stand for healthfulness and have entered the jargon of the advertising industry. Raw, coarse, dark, crunchy, and cloudy foods are preferred over those which are cooked, refined, white, soft, and clear. (See chart.)

Thus dark bread is preferred over white, raw milk over pasteurized, brown rice over white. The convert must learn to eat foods which at first seem strange and even exotic and to reject many foods which are components of the Standard American diet. A McDonald's hamburger, for example, which is an important symbol of America itself (Kottack, 1978), falls into the category of "junk food" and must be rejected.

Just as the magazines and books which articulate the principles of the health food movement and serve as a guide to the convert can be said to comprise the sacred writings of the movement, so the health food store or health food restaurant is the temple where the purity of the movement is guarded and maintained. There individuals find for sale the types of food and other substances advocated by the movement. One does not expect to find items of questionable purity, that is, substances which are not natural or which may be detrimental to health. Within the precincts of the temple adherents can feel safe from the contaminating forces of the larger society, can meet fellow devotees, and can be instructed by the guardians of the sacred area (see, for example, Hongladarom, 1976). Health food stores may vary in their degree of purity. Some sell items such as coffee, raw sugar, or "natural" ice cream which are considered questionable by others of the faith. (One health food store I visited had a sign explaining that it did not sell vitamin supplements, which it considered to be "unnatural," i.e. impure.)

People in other places are often viewed as living more "naturally" and healthfully than contemporary Americans. Observation of such peoples may be used to confirm practices of the movement and to acquire ideas about food. Healthy and long-lived people like the Hunza of the Himalayas are studied to determine the secrets of their strength and longevity. Cultures as yet untainted by the food systems of industrialized nations are seen as examples of what better diet can do. In addition, certain foods from other cultures—foods such as humus, falafel, and tofu—have been adopted into the health food repertoire because of their presumed healthful qualities.

Peoples of other times can also serve as models for a more health-

HEALTH FOOD WORLD VIEW

	Health Foods	Junk Foods	
cosmic oppositions	LIFE NATURE	DEATH CULTURE	
basic values and desirable attributes	holistic, organic harmony with body and nature natural and real harmony, self-sufficiency, independence homemade, small scale layman competence and understanding	fragmented, mechanistic working against body and nature manufactured and artificial disharmony, dependence mass-produced professional esoteric knowledge and jargon	undesirabl attributes
beneficial qualities of food	whole coarse dark crunchy raw cloudy	processed refined white soft cooked clear	harmful qualities
specific foods with mana	yogurt* honey* carob soybeans* sprouts* fruit juices herb teas foods from other cultures: humus, falafel, kefir, tofu, stir-fried vegetables, pita bread	ice cream, candy sugar* chocolate beef overcooked vegetables soft drinks* coffee,* tea "all-American" foods: hot dogs, McDonald's ham- burgers,* potato chips, Coke	specific taboo foods
	return to early American value "real" American way of life	corruption of this original and better way of life and values	

*denotes foods with especially potent mana or taboo.

ful way of life. There is in the health food movement a concept of a "golden age," a past which provides an authority for a better way of living. This past may be scrutinized for clues about how to improve contemporary American society. An archaeologist, writing for *Prevention* magazine, recounts how "I Put Myself on a Caveman Diet—Permanently" (*Prevention*, September 1979). His article explains how he improved his health by utilizing the regular exercise and simpler foods which he had concluded from his research were probably characteristic of our prehistoric ancestors. A general nostalgia about the past seems to exist in the health food movement, along with the feeling that we have departed from a more natural pattern of eating practiced by earlier generations of Americans (see, for example, Hongladarom, 1976). (Sylvester Graham, however, presumably did not find the eating habits of his contemporaries to be very admirable.)

The health food movement is concerned with more than the achievement of bodily health. Nutritional problems are often seen as being at the root of emotional, spiritual, and even social problems. An article entitled "Sugar Neurosis" states "Hypoglycemia (low blood sugar) is a medical reality that can trigger wife-beating, divorce, even suicide" (*Prevention*, April 1979: 110). Articles and books claim to show the reader how to overcome depression through vitamins and nutrition and the movement promises happiness and psychological well-being as well as physical health. Social problems, too, may respond to the health food approach. For example, a probation officer recounts how she tried changing offenders' diets in order to change their behavior. Testimonials from two of the individuals helped tell "what it was like to find that good nutrition was their bridge from the wrong side of the law and a frustrated, unhappy life to a vibrant and useful one" (*Prevention*, May 1978: 56). Thus, through more healthful eating and a more natural lifestyle, the health food movement offers its followers what many religions offer: salvation—in this case salvation for the body, for the psyche, and for society.

Individual effort is the keystone of the health food movement. An individual can take responsibility for his or her own health and does not need to rely on professional medical practitioners. The corollary of this is that it is a person's own behavior which may be the cause of ill health. By sinning, by not listening to our bodies, and by not following a natural way of life, we bring our ailments upon ourselves.

The health food movement also affirms the validity of each individual's experience. No two individuals are alike: needs for different vitamins vary widely; some people are more sensitive to food additives than others; each person has his or her best method of achieving happiness. Therefore, the generalized expertise of professionals and the scientifically verifiable findings of the experts may not be adequate guides for you, the individual, in the search of health. Each person's experience has meaning; if something works for you, then it works. If it works for others also, so much the better, but if it does not, that does not invalidate your own experience. While the movement does not by any means disdain all scientific findings (and indeed they are used extensively when they bolster health food positions), such findings are not seen as the only source of confirmation for the way of life which the health food movement advocates, and the scientific establishment itself tends to be suspect.

In line with its emphasis on individual responsibility for health, the movement seeks to deprofessionalize knowledge and place in every individual's hands the information and means to heal. Drugs used by doctors are usually available only through prescription, but foods and vitamins can be obtained by anyone. Books, magazines, and health food store personnel seek to educate their clientele in ways of healing themselves and maintaining their own health. Articles explain bodily processes, the effects of various substances on health, and the properties of foods and vitamins.

The focus on individual responsibility is frequently tied to a wider concern for self-sufficiency and self-reliance. Growing your own organic garden, grinding your own flour, or even, as one pamphlet suggests, raising your own cow are not simply ways that one can be assured of obtaining healthful food; they are also expressions of independence and self-reliance. Furthermore, such practices are seen as characteristic of an earlier "golden age" when people lived natural lives. For example, an advertisement for vitamins appearing in a digest distributed in health food stores shows a mother and daughter kneading bread together. The heading reads "America's discovering basics." The copy goes on, "Baking bread at home has been a basic family practice throughout history. The past several decades, however, have seen a shift in the American diet to factory-produced breads . . . Fortunately, today there are signs that more and more Americans are discovering the advantage of baking bread themselves." Homemade bread, home-canned produce, sprouts growing on the window sill symbolize what are felt to be basic American values, values supposedly predominant in earlier times when people not only lived on self-sufficient farms and produced their own fresh and more natural food, but also stood firmly on their own two feet and took charge of their own lives. A reader writing to *Prevention* praises an article about a man who found "new life at ninety without lawyers or doctors," saying "If that isn't the optimum in the American way of living, I can't imagine what is!" (*Prevention*, May 1978: 16). Thus although it criticizes the contemporary American way of life, (and although some vegetarians turn to Eastern religions for guidance—see Kandel and Pelto, 1980) the health food movement in general claims to be the true faith, the proponent of basic American-ness, a faith from which the society as a whole has strayed.

SOCIAL SIGNIFICANCE OF THE HEALTH FOOD
MOVEMENT FOR AMERICAN ACTORS

Being a "health food person" involves more than simply changing one's diet or utilizing an alternative medical system. Kandel and Pelto suggest that the health food movement derives much of its popularity from the fact that "Food may be used simultaneously to cure or prevent illness, as a religious symbol and to forge social bonds. Frequently health food users are trying to improve their health, their lives, and, sometimes the world as well" (1980: 332). Use of health foods becomes an affirmation of certain values and a commitment to a certain world view. A person who becomes involved in the health food movement might be said to experience what anthropologist Anthony F. C. Wallace has called "mazeway resynthesis." The "mazeway" is the mental "map" or image of the world which each individual holds. It includes values, the environment and the objects in it, the image of the self and of others, and the techniques one uses to manipulate the environment to achieve desired end states (Wallace, 1970: 237). Resynthesis of this mazeway—that is, the creation of new "maps," values and techniques—commonly occurs in times of religious revitalization, when new religious movements are begun and converts to them are made. As individuals, these converts learn to view the world in a new manner and to act accordingly. In the case of the health food movement, those involved learn to see their health problems and other dissatisfactions with their lives as stemming from improper diet and living in disharmony with nature. They are provided with new values, new ways of viewing their environment, and new techniques for achieving their goals. For such individuals, health food use can come to imply "a major redefinition of self-image, role, and one's relationship to others" (Kandel and Pelto, 1980: 359). The world comes to "make sense" in the light of this new world view. Achievement of the desired end states of better health and an improved outlook on life through following the precepts of the movement gives further validation.

It is this process which gives the health food movement some of the overtones of a religion. As does any new faith, the movement criticizes the prevailing social values and institutions, in this case the health-threatening features of modern industrial society. While an individual's initial dissatisfaction with prevailing beliefs and practices may stem from experiences with the conventional medical system (for example, failure to find a solution to a health problem through visits to a physician), this dissatisfaction often comes to encompass other facets of the American way of life. This further differentiates the "health food person" from mainstream American society (even when the difference is justified as a return to "real" American values).

In everyday life the consumption of such substances as honey, yogurt, and wheat germ, which have come to symbolize the health food movement, does more than contribute to health. It also serves to represent commitment to the health food world view. Likewise, avoiding those substances, such as sugar and white bread, which are considered "evil" is also a mark of a health food person. Ridding the kitchen of such items—a move often advocated by articles advising readers on how to "convert" successfully to health foods—is an act of ritual as well as practical significance. The symbolic nature of such foods is confirmed by the reactions of outsiders to those who are perceived as being inside the movement. An individual who is perceived as being a health food person is often automatically assumed to use honey instead of sugar, for example. Conversely, if one is noticed using or not using certain foods (e.g., adding wheat germ to food, not eating white sugar), this can lead to questions from the observer as to whether or not that individual is a health food person (or a health food "nut," depending upon the questioner's own orientation).

The symbolic nature of such foods is especially important for the health food neophyte. The adoption of a certain way of eating and the renunciation of mainstream cultural food habits can constitute "bridge-burning acts of commitment" (Kendel and Pelto, 1980: 395), which function to cut the individual off from previous patterns of behavior. However, the symbolic activity which indicates this cutting off need not be as radical as a total change of eating habits. In an interview in *Prevention*, a man who runs a health oriented television program recounted an incident in which a viewer called up after a show and announced excitedly that the had changed his whole lifestyle—he had started using honey in his coffee! (*Prevention*, February 1979: 89). While recognizing the absurdity of the action on a practical level, the program's host acknowledged the symbolic importance of this action to the person involved. He also saw it as a step in the right direction since one change can lead to another. Those who sprinkle wheat germ on cereal, toss alfalfa sprouts with a salad, or pass up an ice cream cone for yogurt are not only demonstrating a concern for health but also affirming their commitment to a particular lifestyle and symbolizing adherence to a set of values and a world view.

CONCLUSION

As this analysis has shown, health foods are more than simply a way of eating and more than an alternative healing system. If we return to Clifford Geertz's definition of religion as a "system of symbols" which produces "powerful, pervasive, and long-lasting moods and motivations" by "formulating conceptions of a general order of existence" and making them appear "uniquely realistic," we see that the health food movement definitely has a religious dimension. There is, first, a system of symbols, in this case based on certain kinds and qualities of food. While the foods are believed to have health-giving properties in themselves, they also symbolize a world view which is concerned with the right way to live one's life and the right way to construct a society. This "right way" is based on an approach to life which stresses harmony with nature and the holistic nature of the body. Consumption of those substances designated as "health foods," as well as participation in other activities associated with the movement which also symbolize its world view (such as exercising or growing an organic garden) can serve to establish the "moods and motivations" of which Geertz speaks. The committed health food follower may come to experience a sense of spiritual as well as physical well-being when he or she adheres to the health food way of life. Followers are thus motivated to persist in this way of life, and they come to see the world view of this movement as correct and "realistic."

In addition to its possession of sacred symbols and its "convincing" world view, the health food movement also has other elements which we usually associate with a religion. Concepts of mana and taboo guide the choice of foods. There is a distinction between the pure and impure and a concern for the maintenance of purity. There are "temples" (health food stores and other such establishments) which are expected to maintain purity within their confines. There are "rabbis," or experts in the "theology" of the movement and its application to everyday life. There are sacred and instructional writings which set out the principles of the movement and teach followers how to utilize them. In addition, like many religious movements, the health food movement harkens back to a "golden age" which it seeks to recreate and assumes that many of the ills of the contemporary world are caused by society's departure from this ideal state.

Individuals entering the movement, like individuals entering any religious movement, may undergo a process of conversion. This can be dramatic, resulting from the cure of an illness or the reversal of a previous state of poor health, or it can be gradual, a step by step changing of eating and other habits through exposure to health food doctrine. Individuals who have undergone conversion and mazeway resynthesis, as well as those who have tested and confirmed various aspects of the movement's prescriptions for better health and a better life, may give testimonials to the faith. For those who have adopted, in full or in part, the health food world view, it provides, as do all religions, explanations for existing conditions, answers to specific problems, and a means of gaining control over one's existence. Followers of the movement are also promised "salvation," not in the form of afterlife, but in terms of enhanced physical well-being, greater energy, longer life-span, freedom from illness, and increased peace of mind. However, although the focus is this-worldly, there is a spiritual dimension to the health food movement. And although it does not center its world view around belief in supernatural beings, it does posit a higher authority—the wisdom of nature—as the source of ultimate legitimacy for its views.

Health food people are often dismissed as "nuts" or "food faddists" by those outside the movement. Such a designation fails to recognize the systematic nature of the health food world view, the symbolic significance of health foods, and the important functions which the movement performs for its followers. Health foods offer an alternative or supplement to conventional medical treatment, and a meaningful and effective way for individuals to bring about changes in lives which are perceived as unsatisfactory because of poor physical and emotional health. It can also provide for its followers a framework of meaning which transcends individual problems. In opposign itself to the predominant American lifestyle, the health food movement sets up a symbolic system which opposes harmony to disharmony, purity to pollution, nature to culture, and ultimately, as in many religions, life to death. Thus while foods are the beginning point and the most important symbols of the health food movement, food is not the ultimate focus but rather a means to an end: the organization of a meaningful world view and the construction of a satisfying life.

References

Ehrenreich, Barbara and Deidre English, 1979, *For Her Own Good: 150 Years of the Experts' Advice to Women.* Garden City, New York: Anchor Press/ Doubleday.

Geertz, Clifford, 1965, "Religion as a Cultural System." In Michael Banton, ed., *Anthropological Approaches to the Study of Religion.* ASA Monograph #3. New York: Frederick A. Praeger.

Hongladarom, Gail Chapman, 1976, *Health Seeking Within the Health Food Movement.* Ph.D. dissertation, University of Washington. (Xerox University Microfilms, Ann Arbor.)

Kandel, Randy F. and Gretel H. Pelto, 1980, "The Health Food Movement: Social Revitalization or Alternative Health Maintenance System." In Norge W. Jerome, Randy F. Kandel, and Gretel H. Pelto, eds., *Nutritional Anthropology.* Pleasantville, New York: Redgrave Publishing Company.

Kline, Monte, 1978, *The Junk Food Withdrawal Manual.* Total Life, Inc.

Kottak, Conrad, 1978, "McDonald's as Myth, Symbol and Ritual." In *Anthropology: The Study of Human Diversity.* New York: Random House.

Shryock, Richard Harrison, 1966, *Medicine in America: Historical Essays.* Baltimore: Johns Hopkins.

Wallace, Anthony F. C., 1966, *Religion: An Anthropological View.* New York: Random House.

In 1975, I introduced a unit on religion and ritual into my summer school course in Introductory Anthropology. Much to my surprise, the students in my class began to talk about places like McDonald's and phone booths and gas stations in terms of their ritual aspects. Despite my ongoing commitments to writing about fieldwork I had already conducted in Brazil and Madagascar, I realized that it might be worthwhile to take some time to look at what goes on in these places. This essay is one of the results.

RITUALS AT McDONALD'S
CONRAD P. KOTTAK

The world is blessed each day, on the average, with the opening of a new McDonald's restaurant. They now number more than 4,000 and dot not only the United States but also such countries as Mexico, Japan, Australia, England, France, Germany, and Sweden. The expansion of this international web of franchises and company-owned outlets has been fast and efficient; a little more than twenty years ago McDonald's was limited to a single restaurant in San Bernardino, California. Now, the number of McDonald's outlets has far outstripped the total number of fast-food chains operative in the United States thirty years ago.

McDonald's sales reached $1.3 billion in 1972, propelling it past Kentucky Fried Chicken as the world's largest fast-food chain. It has kept this position ever since. Annual sales now exceed $3 billion. McDonald's is the nation's leading buyer of processed potatoes and fish. Three hundred thousand cattle die each year as McDonald's customers down another three billion burgers. A 1974 advertising budget of $60 million easily made the chain one of the country's top advertisers. Ronald McDonald, our best-known purveyor of hamburgers, French fries, and milk shakes, rivals Santa Claus and Mickey Mouse as our children's most familiar fantasy character.

How does an anthropologist, accustomed to explaining the life styles of diverse cultures, interpret these peculiar developments and attractions that influence the daily life of so many Americans? Have factors other than low cost, taste, fast service, and cleanliness—all of which are approximated by other chains—contributed to McDonald's success? Could it be that in consuming McDonald's products and propaganda, Americans are not just eating and watching television but are experiencing something comparable in some respects to a religious ritual? A brief consideration of the nature of ritual may answer the latter question.

Several key features distinguish ritual from other behavior, according to anthropologist Roy Rappaport. Foremost are formal ritual events—stylized, repetitive, and stereotyped. They occur in special places, at regular times, and include liturgical orders—set sequences of words and actions laid down by someone other than the current performer.

Rituals also convey information about participants and their cultural traditions. Performed year after year, generation after generation, they translate enduring messages, values, and sentiments into observable action. Although some participants may be more strongly committed than others to the beliefs on which rituals are based, all people who take part in joint public acts signal their acceptance of an order that transcends their status as individuals.

In the view of some anthropologists, including Rappaport himself, such secular institutions as McDonald's are not comparable to rituals. They argue that rituals involve special emotions, nonutilitarian intentions, and supernatural entities that are not characteristic of Americans' participation in McDonald's. But other anthropologists define ritual more broadly. Writing about football in contemporary America, William Arens (see "The Great American Football Ritual") points out that behavior can simultaneously have sacred as well as secular aspects. Thus, on one level, football can be interpreted simply as a sport, while on another, it can be viewed as a public ritual.

While McDonald's is definitely a mundane, secular institution— just a place to eat—it also assumes some of the attributes of a sacred place. And in the context of comparative religion, why should this be surprising? The French sociologist Emile Durkheim long ago pointed out that some societies worship the ridiculous as well as the sublime. The distinction between the two does not depend on the intrinsic qualities of the sacred symbol. Durkheim found that Australian aborigines often worshipped such humble and nonimposing creatures as ducks, frogs, rabbits, and grubs—animals whose inherent qualities hardly could have been the origin of the religious sentiment they inspired. If frogs and grubs can be elevated to a sacred level, why not McDonald's?

I frequently eat lunch—and, occasionally, breakfast and dinner— at McDonald's. More than a year ago, I began to notice (and have subsequently observed more carefully) certain ritual behavior at these fast-food restaurants. Although for natives, McDonald's seems to be just a place to eat, careful observation of what goes on in any outlet in this country reveals an astonishing degree of formality and behavioral uniformity on the part of both staff and customers. Particularly impressive is the relative invariance in act and utterance that has developed in the absence of a distinct theological doctrine. Rather, the ritual aspect of McDonald's rests on twentieth-century technology—particularly automobiles, television, work locales, and the one-hour lunch.

The changes in technology and work organization that have contributed to the chain's growth in the United States are now taking place in other countries. Only in a country such as France, which has an established and culturally enshrined cuisine that hamburgers and fish fillets cannot hope to displace, is McDonald's expansion likely to be retarded. Why has McDonald's been so much more successful than other businesses, than the United States Army, and even than many religious institutions in producing behavioral invariance?

Remarkably, even Americans traveling abroad in countries noted for their distinctive food usually visit the local McDonald's outlet. This odd behavior is probably caused by the same factors that urge us to make yet another trip to a McDonald's here. Wherever a McDonald's may be located, it is a home away from home. At any outlet, Americans know how to behave, what to expect, what they will eat, and what they will pay. If one has been unfortunate enough to have partaken of the often indigestible pap dished out by any turnpike restaurant monopoly, the sight of a pair of McDonald's golden arches may justify a detour off the highway, even if the penalty is an extra toll.

In Paris, where the French have not been especially renowned for making tourists feel at home, McDonald's offers sanctuary. It is, after all, an American institution, where only Americans, who are pro-grammed by years of prior experience to salivate at the sight of the glorious hamburger, can feel completely at home. Americans in Paris can temporarily reverse roles with their hosts; if they cannot act like the French, neither can the French be expected to act in a culturally appropriate manner at McDonald's. Away from home, McDonald's, like a familiar church, offers not just hamburgers but comfort, security, and reassurance.

An American's devotion to McDonald's rests in part on unifor-mities associated with almost all McDonald's: setting, architecture, food, ambience, acts, and utterances. The golden arches, for example, serve as a familiar and almost universal landmark, absent only in those areas where zoning laws prohibit garish signs. At a McDonald's near the University of Michigan campus in Ann Arbor, a small, decorous sign—golden arches encircled in wrought iron—identifies the estab-lishment. Despite the absence of the towering arches, this McDonald's, where I have conducted much of my fieldwork, does not suffer as a ritual setting. The restaurant, a contemporary brick struc-ture that has been nominated for a prize in architectural design, is best known for its stained-glass windows, which incorporate golden arches as their focal point. On bright days, sunlight floods in on waiting cus-tomers through a skylight that recalls the clerestory of a Gothic cathe-dral. In the case of this McDonald's, the effect is to equate traditional religious symbols and golden arches. And in the view of the natives I have interviewed, the message is clear.

When Americans go to a McDonald's restaurant, they perform an ordinary, secular, biological act—they eat, usually lunch. Yet im-mediately upon entering, we can tell from our surroundings that we are in a sequestered place, somehow apart from the messiness of the world outside. Except for such anomalies as the Ann Arbor campus outlet, the town house McDonald's in New York City, and the special theme McDonald's of such cities as San Francisco, Saint Paul, and Dallas, the restaurants rely on their arches, dull brown brick, plate-glass sides, and mansard roofs to create a setting as familiar as home. In some of the larger outlets, murals depicting "McDonaldland" fantasy characters, sports, outdoor activities, and landscapes surround plastic seats and tables. In this familiar setting, we do not have to consider the experience. We know what we will see, say, eat, and pay.

Behind the counter, McDonald's employees are differentiated into such categories as male staff, female staff, and managers. While costumes vary slightly from outlet to outlet and region to region, such apparel as McDonald's hats, ties, and shirts, along with dark pants and shining black shoes, are standard.

The food is also standard, again with only minor regional variations. (Some restaurants are selected to test such new menu items as "McChicken" or different milk shake flavors.) Most menus, however, from the rolling hills of Georgia to the snowy plains of Minnesota, offer the same items. The prices are also the same and the menu is usually located in the same place in every restaurant.

Utterances across each spotless counter are standardized. Not only are customers limited in what they can choose but also in what they can say. Each item on the menu has its appropriate McDonald's designation: "quarter pounder with cheese" or "filet-O-fish" or "large fries." The customer who asks, "What's a Big Mac?" is as out of place as a southern Baptist at a Roman Catholic Mass.

At the McDonald's that I frequent, the phrases uttered by the salespeople are just as standard as those of the customers. If I ask for a quarter pounder, the ritual response is "Will that be with cheese, sir?" If I do not order French fries, the agent automatically incants, "Will there be any fries today, sir?" And when I pick up my order, the agent conventionally says, "Have a nice day, sir," followed by, "Come in again."

Nonverbal behavior of McDonald's agents is also programmed. Prior to opening the spigot of the drink machine, they fill paper cups with ice exactly to the bottom of the golden arches that decorate them. As customers request food, agents look back to see if the desired item is available. If not, they reply, "That'll be a few minutes, sir (or ma'am)," after which the order of the next customer is taken.

McDonald's lore of appropriate verbal and nonverbal behavior is even taught at a "seminary," Hamburger University, located in Elk Grove Village, Illinois, near Chicago's O'Hare airport. Managers who attend choose either a two-week basic "operator's course" or an eleven-day "advanced operator's course." With a 360-page *Operations Manual* as their bible, students learn about food, equipment, and management techniques—delving into such esoteric subjects as buns, shortening, and carbonization. Filled with the spirit of McDonald's, graduates take home such degrees as bachelor or master of hamburgerology to display in their outlets. Their job is to spread the word—the secret success formula they have learned—among assistant managers and crew in their restaurants.

The total McDonald's ambience invites comparison with sacred places. The chain stresses clean living and reaffirms those traditional American values that transcend McDonald's itself. Max Boas and Steve Chain, biographers of McDonald's board chairman, Ray Kroc, report that after the hundredth McDonald's opened in 1959, Kroc leased a plane to survey likely sites for the chain's expansion. McDonald's would invade the suburbs by locating its outlets near traffic intersections, shopping centers, and churches. Steeples figured prominently in Kroc's plan. He believed that suburban churchgoers would be pre-programmed consumers of the McDonald's formula—quality, service, and cleanliness.

McDonald's restaurants, nestled beneath their transcendent arches and the American flag, would enclose immaculate restrooms and floors, counters and stainless steel kitchens. Agents would sparkle, radiating health and warmth. Although to a lesser extent than a decade ago, management scrutinizes employees' hair length, height, nails, teeth, and complexions. Long hair, bad breath, stained teeth, and pimples are anathema. Food containers also defy pollution; they are used only once. (In New York City, the fast-food chain Chock Full O' Nuts foreshadowed this theme long ago and took it one step further by assuring customers that their food was never touched by human hands.)

Like participation in rituals, there are times when eating at McDonald's is not appropriate. A meal at McDonald's is usually confined to ordinary, everyday life. Although the restaurants are open virtually every day of the year, most Americans do not go there on Thanksgiving, Easter, Passover, or other religious and quasi-religious days. Our culture reserves holidays for family and friends. Although Americans neglect McDonald's on holidays, the chain reminds us through television that it still endures, that it will welcome us back once our holiday is over.

The television presence of McDonald's is particularly obvious on holidays, whether it be through the McDonald's All-American Marching Band (two clean-cut high school students from each state) in a nationally televised Thanksgiving Day parade or through sponsorship of sports and family entertainment programs.

Although such chains as Burger King, Burger Chef, and Arby's compete with McDonald's for the fast-food business, none rivals McDonald's success. The explanation reflects not just quality, service, cleanliness, and value but, more importantly, McDonald's advertising, which skillfully appeals to different audiences. Saturday morning television, for example, includes a steady dose of cartoons and other children's shows sponsored by McDonald's. The commercials feature several McDonaldland fantasy characters, headed by the clown Ronald McDonald, and often stress the enduring aspects of McDonald's. In one, Ronald has a time machine that enables him to introduce hamburgers to the remote past and the distant future. Anyone who noticed the shot of the McDonald's restaurant in the Woody Allen film *Sleeper*, which takes place 200 years hence, will be aware that the message of McDonald's as eternal has gotten across. Other children's commercials gently portray the conflict between good (Ronald) and evil (Hamburglar). McDonaldland's bloblike Grimace is hooked on milk shakes, and Hamburglar's addiction to simple burgers regularly culminates in his confinement to a "patty wagon," as Ronald and Big Mac restore and preserve the social order.

Pictures of McDonaldland appear on cookie boxes and, from time to time, on durable plastic cups that are given away with the purchase of a large soft drink. According to Boas and Chain, a McDonaldland amusement park, comparable in scale to Disneyland, is planned for Las Vegas. Even more obvious are children's chances to meet Ronald McDonald and other McDonaldland characters in the flesh. Actors portraying Ronald scatter their visits, usually on Saturdays, among McDonald's outlets throughout the country. A Ronald can even be rented for a birthday party or for Halloween trick or treating.

McDonald's adult advertising has a different, but equally effective, theme. In 1976, a fresh-faced, sincere young woman invited the viewer to try breakfast—a new meal at McDonald's—in a familiar setting. In still other commercials, healthy, clean-living Americans gambol on ski slopes or in mountain pastures. The single theme running throughout all the adult commercials is personalism. McDonald's, the commercials tell us, is not just a fast-food restaurant. It is a warm, friendly place where you will be graciously welcomed. Here, you will feel at home with your family, and your children will not get into trouble. The word *you* is emphasized—"You deserve a break today"; "You, you're the one"; "We do it all for you." McDonald's commercials say that you are not simply a face in a crowd. At McDonald's, you can find respite from a hectic and impersonal society—the break you deserve.

Early in 1977, after a brief flirtation with commercials that harped on the financial and gustatory benefits of eating at McDonald's, the chain introduced one of its more curious incentives—the "Big Mac attack." Like other extraordinary and irresistible food cravings, which people in many cultures attribute to demons or other spirits, a Big Mac attack could strike anyone at any time. In one commercial, passengers on a jet forced the pilot to land at the nearest McDonald's. In others, a Big Mac attack had the power to give life to an inanimate object, such as a suit of armor, or restore a mummy to life.

McDonald's advertising typically de-emphasizes the fact that the chain is, after all, a profit-making organization. By stressing its program of community projects, some commercials present McDonald's as a charitable organization. During the Bicentennial year, commercials reported that McDonald's was giving 1,776 trees to every state in the union. Brochures at outlets echo the television message that, through McDonald's, one can sponsor a carnival to aid victims of muscular dystrophy. In 1976 and 1977 McDonald's managers in Ann Arbor persuaded police officers armed with metal detectors to station themselves at restaurants during Halloween to check candy and fruit for hidden pins and razor blades. Free coffee was offered to parents. In 1976, McDonald's sponsored a radio series documenting the contributions Blacks have made to American history.

McDonald's also sponsored such family television entertainment as the film *The Sound of Music,* complete with a prefatory, sermonlike address by Ray Kroc. Commercials during the film showed Ronald McDonald picking up after litterbugs and continued with the theme, "We do it all for you." Other commercials told us that McDonald's supports and works to maintain the values of American family life—and went so far as to suggest a means of strengthening what most Americans conceive to be the weakest link in the nuclear family, that of father-child. "Take a father to lunch," kids were told.

Participation in McDonald's rituals involves temporary subordination of individual differences in a social and cultural collectivity. By eating at McDonald's, not only do we communicate that we are hungry, enjoy hamburgers, and have inexpensive tastes but also that we are willing to adhere to a value system and a series of behaviors dictated by an exterior entity. In a land of tremendous ethnic, social, economic, and religious diversity, we proclaim that we share something with millions of other Americans.

Sociologists, cultural anthropologists, and others have shown that social ties based on kinship, marriage, and community are growing weaker in the contemporary United States. Fewer and fewer people participate in traditional organized religions. By joining sects, cults, and therapy sessions, Americans seek many of the securities that formal religion gave to our ancestors. The increasing cultural, rather than just economic, significance of McDonald's, football, and similar institutions is intimately linked to these changes.

As industrial society shunts people around, church allegiance declines as a unifying moral force. Other institutions are also taking over the functions of formal religions. At the same time, traditionally organized religions—Protestantism, Catholicism, and Judaism—are reorganizing themselves along business lines. With such changes, the gap between the symbolic meaning of traditional religions and the realities of modern life widens. Because of this, some sociologists have argued that the study of modern religion must merge with the study of mass culture and mass communication.

In this context, McDonald's has become one of the many new and powerful elements of American culture that provide common expectations, experience, and behavior—overriding region, class, formal religious affiliation, political sentiments, gender, age, ethnic group, sexual preference, and urban, suburban, or rural residence. By incorporating—wittingly or unwittingly—many of the ritual and symbolic aspects of religion, McDonald's has carved its own important niche in a changing society in which automobiles are ubiquitous and where television sets outnumber toilets.

My interest is in what I call "personal anthropology," the effort to relate anthropological concepts and methods to the student's everyday life situation. Anthropology becomes more personal and meaningful to the undergraduate if it takes as its subject matter the world of the student. The graffiti research that Jan Kelso and I did together illustrates these points, and shows that systematic study of a commonplace subject, scribblings on the walls of toilet stalls, will yield enhanced awareness of social processes. It is essential, however, to go beyond the surface level to an anthropological analysis of the data if the underlying message is to be revealed. The aim is to develop a reflexive view, and to acquire the skills necessary to analyze everyday experience with the techniques of the social sciences. I challenge the readers to take the methodology of this paper and to conduct an investigation of the toilet graffiti on their own campus.

GENDER DIFFERENCES IN GRAFFITI
A Semiotic Perspective

EDWARD M. BRUNER
and
JANE PAIGE KELSO

SYNOPOSIS

Male and female restroom graffiti are analyzed from a semiotic perspective for what they reveal about processes of communication in same sex encounters. The meaning of the lavatory inscriptions are examined on the manifest and underlying levels. The gender differences that emerge are interpreted as basically political, as an effort to deal with problems of power and stratification in American society.

INTRODUCTION

Studies of restroom graffiti conducted over the past twenty-five years by different investigators point to a similar conclusion—that inscriptions written by men are different in essential respects from those written by women (Kinsey et al., 1953; Dundes, 1966; Landy and Steele, 1967; Martilla, 1971; Stocker et al., 1972; Solomon and Yager, 1975; Wales and Brewer, 1976; Reich et al., 1977; Peretti et al., 1977; Alexander, 1978; Greenberg, 1979). The same finding emerged from a recent study we carried out on our own campus.[2] Taken together, these studies raise two major questions: how do we characterize male-female differences in graffiti and what is the meaning of these differences? In this paper we report upon the results of our study guided by these questions.

One impediment to an appreciation of the significance of gender differences in *latrinalia*[3] has been the multiplicity of disciplines involved. Data on restroom graffiti have been gathered by scholars in folklore, psychology, psychiatry, sociology, and anthropology and have been reported upon in widely scattered journals (see for example Sechrest and Flores, 1969; Sechrest and Olson, 1971; Gadpaille, 1971; Lomas, 1973; Gonos et al., 1976; Abel and Buckley, 1977; Longenecker, 1977; Asher, 1979). There are distinct disciplinary traditions in graffiti research. Such recent descriptions of gender differences as Wales and Brewer (1976), Reich et all. (1977), Peretti et al. (1977) and Alexander (1978) do not cite a single reference in common.

The first study refers only to the graffiti literature in psychology, the second to folklore, the third to historical accounts and popular works, and the last to sociology. It is understandable that these studies do not refer to each other, as all appeared in print at approximately the same time, but it is striking that the references in the four papers are entirely different. The individual scholars, of course, have legitimate disciplinary concerns and ask questions of the graffiti data relevant to their own field of interest. Such independence may lend credibility to the results, but it detracts from the cumulative impact of the findings.

The literature on restroom graffiti may be segmented into two major types that we call the positivist and the psychoanalytic. The two differ in a number of dimensions but the most important for our purposes is in how they handle meaning. To anticipate our critique, the positivist studies suffer from an underattribution of meaning, whereas the psychoanalytic studies suffer from an overattribution. Each approach utilizes a different theory of the text and of the role of interpretation, and hence they handle meaning differently.

The positivists begin with a corpus of graffiti writings gathered from male and female restrooms, devise a set of content categories, and then assign each individual graffito to a category. After all the graffiti have been classified they count the number of items in each category, construct a frequency distribution, and perform tests for statistical significance. The discussion is then conducted in terms of those categories for which there are significant gender differences, as determined by the statistical tests. Wales and Brewer (1976:118-119) provide an example of the kind of categories employed: racial insults, sexual insults, racial/sexual insults, general insults, sexual humor, general humor, sexual request, sexual or scatological words, romantic, general racial, political, drugs, religion, morals, names, and miscellaneous. The sixteen categories are exclusive as each graffito is counted only once.

We have three objections to the positivist approach. The first is that the categories selected seem arbitrary and in any case there is rarely discussion of the rationale for the system of categorization. One study uses three major categories, another five, and still another twenty. Our second objection is that the approach breaks down the data into isolated elements which blur the underlying patterning involved. Gender differences are reduced to a statistical counting which slices up and destroys whatever structure may be present. Our most serious objection, however, is that, although the scientific procedures may be impeccable, one is never entirely sure of the meaning of the findings (see for example Greenberg, 1979:268). All positivist studies agree that gender differences exist, but the meaning of these differences is not taken as problematic. To put it another way, there is an implicit theory of text which assumes that the meaning is the message, and that significance will be revealed by counting the frequency with which items of manifest content appear. The graffiti mean what the graffiti say, without any attempt to interpret the text. In ordinary social life and in reading any form of drama we are very much aware of the discrepancy between what the words say and what they mean, and in order to understand we must engage in an act of interpretation. The positivist studies, however, take a very literal empiricist approach.

The psychoanalysts, on the other hand, do go beyond the manifest text to a meaningful interpretation on a deeper level. The problem with psychoanalytic studies, however, is that one is never entirely sure of the relationship between graffiti inscriptions and the interpretation that is offered. It is as if the Freudians have a stock set of meanings involving unconscious impulses, infantile sexuality, and primitive thoughts which are attributed to various bodies of data, including graffiti. All too often, the connection between the data and the Freudian meaning is not readily apparent. In this sense, we say that psychoanalytic approaches suffer from an overattribution of meaning compared to the underattribution of positivist social science. Possibly a more serious deficiency of psychoanalytic theory is that while it may fit male graffiti it seems entirely inappropriate as an explanation of female inscriptions, as we will demonstrate below.

What then is our perspective? In this paper we take a semiotic approach beginning with the recognition that restroom graffiti is communication, a silent conversation among anonymous partners. Although written in the privacy of a toilet stall, the writing of graffiti is an essentially social act that cannot be understood in terms of the expressive functions performed for an isolated individual. To write graffiti is to communicate; one never finds graffiti where it cannot be seen by others. A new person coming to a toilet stall who chooses to write a graffito must take account of what has previously been written, even in the minimal sense of choosing an appropriate location on the wall, and a message is left for those who will subsequently come to that stall. The identity of those engaged in the discourse is never revealed, and all the exchanges occur while one is engaged in the act of voiding or defecating. It is indeed a very unique form of communication, almost a limiting case. The graffiti writings build up on the walls until an anonymous janitor comes in the night to wipe it all away, and the cycle of the silent discourse begins again the following day.

The most crucial aspect of restroom graffiti from our perspective is that it is same-sex communication. Given the segregation of restrooms in American culture, male graffiti is written by men for other men, and female graffiti is written by women for other women. There are two separate universes of discourse, one for men and another for women. The empirical finding of gender differences in restroom graffiti suggests that communication patterns in same-sex encounters are essentially different. Our approach, then, enables us to relate differences in male and female graffiti to that body of literature dealing with patterns of interaction and communication in same-sex groups (Jenkins and Kramer, 1978). No previous investigator of restroom graffiti has made this connection, but it is basic to the interpretation that we will present.

THE DATA

Before turning to the data itself, we make some conceptual and methodological points that follow from our semiotic perspective. As there are many levels of meaning, we distinguish between the surface text which contains the manifest message and the underlying text at the level of depth semantics. There is meaning or significance at both the surface and underlying levels, and both require interpretation on the part of the analyst. Our criteria of adequacy are that the relationship between the imputed meaning at both levels must be systematic for the male and the female data. We emerge then with the following fourfold paradigm:

male	female
surface	
underlying	

Our objective in the rest of the paper is to fill in the four empty spaces, and we emphasize again that it will not be satisfactory to provide four separate unrelated explanations. The content of the four spaces must be systematically interrelated. Our interpretation of the meaning of gender differences must convincingly demonstrate a clear relationship between male-female on surface-underlying levels.

Our findings were based upon inscriptions copied from restroom walls on our campus and in the adjacent town during spring, 1978. A total of 767 discrete items were recorded, 438 from women's stalls and 329 from men's. We refer to these materials as our primary data. A supplementary source consisted of data collected during fall, 1976 from 64 male restrooms and 37 female restrooms by students in an introductory anthropology class.[4] Further, a questionnaire was placed on the PLATO computer system asking such questions as "Why do you think people write graffiti?" and "Can you give an example of the kind of graffiti you write or like to see?" Responses were received from 108 men and 23 women. The computer system was used because the replies were anonymous, as they are for graffiti writers in toilet stalls. It was difficult for us to evaluate these materials—one woman respondent defined graffiti as tiny Italian giraffes—but nevertheless the responses were helpful. Finally, 30 students were interviewed about graffiti. In the presentation of the results that follows we rely upon our primary data; supplementary sources such as the student material, the computer questionnaire, and the interviews; and of course the literature, another excellent source of data and insights.

In our handling of these data we take the linguistic model as a metaphor. A linguist, for example, interested in the difference between the words "bat" and "pat" would say that "at" is common to both and that what is different is "b" and "p," which may be expressed in terms of the binary distinction voiced and not voiced. The method is to isolate the differences and to express them in terms of a relationship. Thus, we focus only on what is different in male-female wall writings rather than with the entire corpus of graffiti data. Our primary objective, of course, is precisely to characterize and explain gender *differences*. As many types of inscriptions found in men's and women's restrooms are similar, we do not deal with them. These include general questions, invitations, and what the folklorist Dundes calls traditional graffiti:

OK Damn it! It's almost spring break. Where are you all off to?

[followed by a long series of responses]

308-693-5493 for a good screw

sex is like bridge—if you have a good hand you don't need a partner

Here I sit, broken hearted
Paid to shit but only farted

An inspection of the surface text reveals that male and female restroom graffiti differ in two major respects. The first is that women's graffiti is more interactive and interpersonal; one woman will raise a question, and others will provide a string of responsive and serious replies. Typical initial questions are as follows:

I love Ray, but he only wants to have a good time. What should I do?

I've never had sexual intercourse before but my boyfriend and I have decided that we want to. He's very experienced and I know nothing. I don't know what to do. Please help me.

Reassure me that morality still has something to do with sex.

Have you ever fallen in love with a guy who screws you over and you didn't know it until it was too late?

I'm in love! "married" "pregnant" happy
Wish this to all of you!

An example of an initial comment with responses is the following:

I am so fortunate. I love. I am loved. I try to be deserving of the good.

—I love and am loved by 2 men. Sharing love is *great*. But I just can't
handle two. What should I do? P.S. I've been with one boy for four
years. I've been with the other six months (I really love them both).

—I can't believe it. I came here to write of the same problem. I, too,
love two men. One is far away one here at school. I have considered
dropping both but my innate (and human) selfishness won't allow it. The
here knows of the other but won't force a decision of me (how could I not
love him!?) I'm leaving it to fate, when I get confused! I think both of
them individually and assuage the competition in my heart between
them. Beyond that I have no solution.

—Oh my God, same here the exact same story to a T. Is this a fad or
something?

—Blow them both off and start over.

As indicated by these examples, women raise serious questions
about such topics as love, how to handle sexual relations, and level of
commitment. They solicit advice, share experiences, write about
specific individuals, and deal with real problems. This kind of graffiti is
simply not found in male restrooms. Men do write sequential graffiti
but they are neither advisory nor serious. A man would be subject to
ridicule if he were to ask "Should I have sex with my girl friend?", even
though the question may be of actual and legitimate concern.

Many inscriptions found in female restrooms are not advisory, but
are shorter "love and romance" graffiti. They occasionally appear in
male restrooms but less frequently. Here are some examples:

I love Doug

Holly loves Bob

I got pinned

In contrast to the caretaking quality of most women's graffiti, the
inscriptions written by men are more self-centered and competitive.

Men write about their sexual conquests, sexual prowess, and frequency of performance. There are graphic descriptions of sex organs separate from the body, and one find over- and underexaggerations of the penis. We found one entire wall in a men's toilet stall covered with a drawing of a gigantic erect ejaculating penis. There was also a picture of a man in the act of castration, cutting off his penis, as well as two separate drawings of black men, one with no penis and another with a very small one. Women's graffiti are more conversational and deal with relationships; men's are more individualistic and deal with isolated sex acts and organs. Abel and Buckley (1977:10) have an excellent summary of the main themes found in male lavatories: male and female genitalia; heterosexual and homosexual behavior; genital, oral, and anal intercourse; products of elimination either in isolation or meant to express hostility toward various persons, races, religions, nationalities, and institutions.

A second major gender difference in graffiti is that 54% of the men's inscriptions were derogatory compared to only 15% of the women's[5] By derogatory we mean any item that is hostile, aggressive, negative, racist or that could be classified as an attack, insult, or "putdown." Here are examples of male derogatory graffiti:

Jews have big noses because the air is free.
—And little dicks because whores cost so much.

Commerce is Jewish engineering

How come Skoki (sic) got the Jews and Evanston got the niggers?
Evanston had first choice.

Q: What do you get when you cross a nigger with an ape?
A: A stupid ape
   A smart nigger
   The best fuck the ape ever had

A couple of years ago, I couldn't understand how Hitler could *kill the Jews* like he did, now I understand!! At the bottom of the lake is shit below that is Jews

—underneath which are niggers

— underneath that are you idiots who write this shit on the walls

shoot queers

fags will burn

Faggots should be castrated then drowned in boiling cat urine

Difference between toilet seats and sorority bitches

—you shit on toilet seats; sorority bitches shit on you

—You're allowed to put something through a toilet seat hole

—Toilet seats have shit below them; sorority bitches have shit all thru them

—no difference

—They both stink

—Toilets have smaller holes and smell better

—you can't get VD from a toilet seat

—Toilet seats are warm

DISCUSSION

Before discussing these data we should like to predict the reactions of the readers of this article to our examples of female advisory and male derogatory graffiti. Obviously this is risky as one never knows in advance who the readers will be, but our prediction is that when men read the female examples they will experience slight surprise at their mildness, and that when women read the male examples they will be shocked at the virulent racism, aggression, and imagery of violence. If our prediction is even partially correct, it indicates something very fundamental about gender differences and about the nature of the graffiti material. Men and women, ordinarily, have an opportunity for only a single "reading" and never know about graffiti in restrooms of the opposite sex. When the issue is raised they are curious; during our interviews with 30 students all but one asked about opposite sex graffiti. The interviews we conducted with individuals and with same-sex groups yielded similar results, but attempted interviews with mixed-sex groups were unsatisfactory as no one would talk freely. When men and women are confronted with the image of the other depicted in restroom graffiti, the situation becomes awkward and embarrassing.

Our findings on the surface pattern of male-female differences in restroom graffiti may be characterized as follows:

Male	Female
egocentric	interpersonal
individualistic	interactive
competitive	advisory
macho	caretaking
sex	love
erotic	romantic
organs	persons
more derogatory	less derogatory

The pattern found in our study is confirmed by other investigators. Alexander (1978:48-49) and Wales and Brewer (1976:120) report conclusions very similar to our own. "Romantic graffiti were almost exclusive female phenomena," Alexander writes (meaning by romantic statements of love or love relationships). He says that "erotic drawings were found exclusively in male rest rooms," with females around to provide a variety of "fleshy semenal repositories." Essentially the same findings were reported by Kinsey (1953:673), although he views male-female differences in graffiti as "basic," implying that they are innate rather than socially constructed. We reject Kinsey's interpretation, but his data are consistent with our findings. He informs us that 86% of male inscriptions and 25% of female writings were erotic and concludes "Most of the female inscriptions referred to love . . . but very few of them were genital or dealt with genital actions or sexual vocabularies."

It might be argued that graffiti are just talk and that all they reveal are traditional idioms. Men use "erotic" words and women "romantic" words, but they really mean the same thing. It is all a question of language, of how men and women have been socialized to express themselves. There is some validity to this position in that gender differences in graffiti do reflect culturally patterned and socially acquired ways of communicating and interacting in same-sex groups. But we would not agree that different words have the same meaning. This is a tricky argument because even if men and women used identical words in their restroom inscriptions we could not be entirely sure if those words had identical meanings. Carol Mitchell (1977) reports that men and women laugh at the same jokes, but for different reasons. In this vein, we believe that men and women experience graffiti in different ways, and that the messages conveyed and the meaning of the graffiti are different. We cannot dismiss twenty-five years of consistent research findings on gender differences in latrinalia as just talk.

It is necessary, however, to make a distinction between the raw data as illustrated by our examples and the words that we and other investigators have used to talk about that body of data. Words such as "advisory," or "individualistic," or any of the binary terms in our summary chart of the surface pattern of gender differences may reflect the literature about graffiti more than the actual inscriptions. One could legitimately take issue with the terms selected. Oppositions such as "love" vs. "sex" are indeed gross characterizations. The word "erotic," which appears throughout the graffiti literature, stems from Kinsey. It was his hypothesis that men find graffiti sexually stimulating while women do not, which is questionable to begin with. But given this supposition, he then described male graffiti as erotic, and other investigators have followed his usage. Even though one may quarrel with the metalanguage used to discuss gender differences in graffiti, those differences do exist. The problem of a suitable metalanguage is one that plagues every scientific discipline.

The data we obtained in interviews and on questionnaires also support our analysis of lavatory inscriptions. Of the women interviewed, over one-quarter mentioned that they enjoy advisory question and answer graffiti; not one man mentioned this topic. Females commented on love/sex themes twice as frequently as males. About 8% of the men said they like racist and anti-Semitic inscriptions; not one woman did so. Of the male respondents to the questionnaire, about 20% stated that one reason people write graffiti is to vent frustrations and to get rid of hostility; only 5% of the females gave a similar reason. In the interviews men made such remarks as "Everyone needs exploding space" and "You have to let it out, right?", whereas female responses referred to less aggressive ways of expressing their feelings. It should also be noted that informant commentary on graffiti can be misleading. Over a third of both men and women indicated that they most appreciated witty, clever, and original graffiti. This may indeed be their preference as readers, but such graffiti does not appear that frequently.

Still another independent confirmation of the validity of our findings is that they are consistent with the growing literature on gender differences in communication. In their recent review Jenkins and Kramer (1978:77) write that "the communication behavior of women has not generally conformed to male models." Rae Carlson (1971:268-269) explores self-other representations and suggests that there are "distinctive masculine and feminine styles, discernible in quite diverse areas." We quote two of Carlson's hypotheses: "1. Males tend to experience and represent the self in individualistic terms; females tend to experience and represent the self in terms of interpersonal relatedness. . . . 2. Males represent others in objective classifying terms; females represent others in subjective, interpretive terms." A study of consciousness raising groups by Susan Kalcik (1975) suggests that women collaborate in storytelling, that their narrative is conversational, and that they collectively develop a kernel story, much like advisory graffiti. Male storytelling is more individualistic in the style of a performer before an audience. Elizabeth Aries (1976) finds that in same-sex groups male stories tend to stress aggressiveness and superiority, whereas female stories deal more with feelings and relationships.

OTHER EXPLANATIONS

To summarize thus far, our findings on gender differences in latrinalia are supported by other investigations conducted over a period of decades, by our own independently gathered interviews and questionnaires, and by others who have studied male-female differences in patterns of communication. Although others have not conceptualized the problem as we have, there is a substantial body of support for our findings from a wide variety of sources. Thus, we may now turn to the explanations of male-female differences in graffiti that have appeared in the literature, after which we shall offer our interpretation of the underlying meaning of these data.

Our first point is that the psychoanalysts simply do not have an explanation of gender differences in graffiti, although Dundes (1966), Gadpaille (1971), Lomas (1973) and Abel and Buckley (1977) have done very insightful work. Their insights, however, illuminate the male data and are simply not applicable to the female inscriptions. Let us develop this argument.

From the psychoanalytic perspective, the model of dream analysis so brilliantly provided by Freud serves as a metaphor for the analysis of graffiti. Wall inscriptions, like dreams, are an "eruption of the unconscious" (Gadpaille, 1971:46). In the state of sleep the censoring mechanisms are relaxed and one's deepest thoughts, buried in the unconscious, are manifested and revealed in the disguised symbolic language of the dream. So it is with restroom graffiti. In the toilet stall, while voiding or defecating, there is an arousal of unconscious associations that are both sexual and aggressive. As the anal area is a zone of sexual excitation the very process of defecation leads to erotic sensations. It is not an accident that "fuck" and "shit" are written so frequently on the walls of toilet stalls, or that sex and excrement are key themes. The expression "fuck you" is clearly sexual and aggressive, and the penis is not only a sexual organ but, like a gun or a knife, is often perceived as a weapon, as an aggressive tool. Feces are unclean, as are all products of the body, and as dirt or polluted substances they are utilized as idioms for the expression of hostility.

The essence of the psychoanalytic position is stated by Lomas (1973:85): "in virtually every case . . . writing on the wall is at bottom the expression of aggressive and destructive wishes." One of our graffiti writers in the section of male examples neatly anticipated this position when he referred to "you idiots who write this shit on the walls." From the psychoanalytic viewpoint, graffiti is "shit" or symbolic dirt and to write a graffito is to smear feces.

Clearly, the psychoanalytic view does apply to erotic derogatory male graffiti with its emphasis on sexual and aggressive themes but it does not help at all with the serious, advisory, interactive female graffiti. Once again, psychoanalytic theory works better for men than for women. We then ask, how is female graffiti viewed from a psychoanalytic perspective? Abel and Buckley (1977:137) tells us it consists mostly "of bland statements" with "very little humor" and Lomas (1973:76) agrees that it is "sparse and unimaginative." There are, however, many current efforts to revise psychoanalytic theory in light of the feminist critique, and in any case blatant sexism is not restricted to any one theoretical position. Bates (quoted in Greenberg, 1979:268), on the basis of a positivist study of gender differences in graffiti at the University of Massachusetts, concludes that women are ". . . sexually confused and humorless individuals, far less able than men to cope with stresses common to the human condition."

A series of hypotheses have been offered by other investigators to explain gender differences but none have been widely accepted or developed. Male-female differences in graffiti for Alexander (1978) reflect social role expectations, for Dundes (1966) male pregnancy envy, and for Kinsey (1953) sex differences in patterns of erotic arousal. These investigators, of course, pose somewhat different questions, conceptualize the problem in their own way, and do not attempt to explain the same phenomena. It has been frequently reported, for example, that men write more graffiti than women (Wales and Brewer, 1976 and Greenberg, 1979 are exceptions), and a variety of reasons have been suggested as to why this should be so. Our interest, however, is not in the quantity of graffiti produced, but in the pattern of gender differences, to which we now turn.

UNDERLYING MEANING

Our interpretation of the underlying meaning of male restroom inscriptions is that they reaffirm male dominance and perpetuate the power structure. We invite the reader to look again at our examples of male derogatory graffiti: they denigrate, in sequence, Jews, blacks, homosexuals, and women. Whatever other covert messages may be contained in male graffiti it is clear that they deal with relations of superordination and subordination, one of the most important sociological aspects of American society. Even the imagery of male inscriptions in our examples refer to layers, strata, comparisons, and contrasts.

Possibly the most fundamental respect in which we differ from previous investigators is that we view the treatment of women in male graffiti as denigrating rather than sexual. The inscriptions in men's restrooms degrade or subordinate on the basis of sex; they are pornographic rather than erotic. Only a very masochistic person would be sexually stimulated by such graffiti, but of course this misses the point—on the surface level male graffiti may deal with sex, but on the covert level it is concerned with power. In other words, women are depicted as another minority or subordinate group, and what has been labeled sexual or erotic graffiti is actually in the same category as racist.

The same point emerges from an examination of the system of categorization used in graffiti research. The coding system, of course, is not simply a methodological problem, but contains an implicit theoretical position. Stocker et al. (1972), for example, have three major categories, heterosexual, homosexual, and nonsexual, and as subcategories of the latter are humorous, hostile, and social satire. Alexander (1978) has thirteen categories including humorous, heterosexual, scatological, and racial-ethnic. We have seen that Wales and Brewer (1976) have such categories as racial insults, sexual insults, sexual humor, and sexual or scatological words. On the surface level one could classify the obvious manifest content as sexual, humorous, satirical, hostile, scatological or racial-ethnic. But look again at our example of male graffiti that asks about the difference between "toilet seats and sorority bitches." Is this sexual, scatological, insulting, humorous or all of the above? We know that jokes may disguise hostility but so may graffiti cast in sexual terms. Classification cease to be a problem for us once we recognized that an anti-Semitic joke, an anti-black racial insult, a hostile comment about gays, and a sexual put-down of women were all simply derogatory, and served to reaffirm the dominance of white males. We are assuming, of course, that Jews, blacks, and homosexuals do not denigrate themselves in graffiti.

The question emerges, why should white males who already have power need to reassert their superordinate position, and why in such a harsh and virulent manner? Why should it be necessary to denigrate peoples that are already dominated? Our answer, in part, is because the subordinate groups are preceived as threatening. On our campus there is a sizeable Jewish contingent from the Chicago suburbs who confront a predominantly WASP student body, many from rural downstate Illinois, who have never interacted with Jews before coming to the university. There is also a large fraternity-sorority system segregated into houses on the basis of sex, religion, and race—men are segregated from women, Jews from gentiles, and blacks from whites. Many white males feel reverse discrimination as good jobs are becoming scarce, and affirmative action programs are prominent on campus and among the corporations that recruit new graduates. The gay liberation group is small but increasingly vocal, and the women's movement is in everyone's consciousness, in part due to the media and the current controversy surrounding ERA.

Although we found that Jews, blacks, homosexuals, and women were the primary objects of derogatory inscriptions, we know that as circumstances change the objects of derogation change accordingly. On our campus, for example, 14% of the men's graffiti was anti-Semitic and 6% was antiblack, but we have data suggesting that on our Chicago campus, with its higher proportion of black students, these percentages would be reversed.[6] Alan Dundes informs us that in male restrooms in Los Angeles he has observed many inscriptions against Arabs and Iranians, indicative of their visibility in southern California, whereas such graffiti were totally absent when we collected our sample. Recently, however, we observed two inscriptions against Iranians. Stocker et al. report that the very high frequency of racial graffiti on the Southern Illinois campus in 1970 had dropped considerably by 1972, after the easing of racial strife in Carbondale and nearby Cairo. During periods of strife and conflict, when men feel most threatened, they direct their most vitriolic remarks against those groups whom they perceive as most challenging. There is no doubt that the objects of aggression fluctuate with the times and with the local competitive situation.

In dealing with these issues it is important to keep our sights on the larger social system and on the overall constellation of power relations. It would be an oversimplification to focus narrowly on such particular issues as blacks vs. whites, or women vs. men. The point is that all the groups are part of a total structure of stratification, and male graffiti reflects that larger structure, *as it is perceived by men.* The graffiti produced by men reflect the subjective concerns and fears experienced by men.

Jews, blacks, homosexuals, and women are oppressed groups in American society, but it is equally clear that no amount of graffiti writing is going to change the actual power relations. Inscriptions on the walls of toilet stalls are not a significant part of our success-oriented competitive society, and the messages they contain are grossly distorted mythological fantasies. What, then, is accomplished by writing them? Men who are struggling with the problem of power and their own role in society gain some measure of mastery by the writing and reading of graffiti. Men write graffiti to tell themselves and other men that they have maintained their superior position and are still in control.

In restroom graffiti, men communicate their deepest concerns about power. The language in which they communicate is a symbolic restroom code, a set of male cultural conventions appropriate to the lavatory. On the surface level one finds a series of sexual and racial slurs written or scratched on the walls of toilet stalls, but on the underlying level we have a silent discourse about power and the American system of stratification. The act of writing graffiti transforms an inner concern into an external object outside the self, located there on the wall, where it may be confronted and mastered. The externalization of inner concerns about power and status in a symbolic common code is what enables men to come to terms with those concerns.

What about women's graffiti and how does it relate to power? We emphasize again that we see women's inscriptions as a separate universe of discourse, one that uses their own cultural code and communicative conventions, and conveys their own messages and meanings. It has been an error of previous research, we believe, to regard male and female graffiti as if they were the same phenomena. To do so ignores the differentiation between male and female forms of communication.

Our view is that women write graffiti that asks for and gives advice primarily about relationships with men because they are subordinate to men—they support one another in their opposition to men. The underlying meaning of female restroom graffiti is that it expresses the cooperation of the dominated and reflects the strategy of mutual help employed by those in a subordinate status. That women's inscriptions are cooperative and helpful should come as no surprise—it is exactly what one would expect among the members of any minority group. It is the rhetoric of "brothers" and "sisters" that one finds among blacks and other minorities. We do not imply that graffiti found in black restrooms would not be derogatory. Black men, even though they are subordinate in the larger society, might well denigrate women.

One way of conceptualizing the differences in the underlying meaning of male and female graffiti is to focus on the verbs used to describe what is happening. Men reaffirm their dominance; women rethink their position. It is generally true in any system of stratification that those on top attempt to maintain and reassert their control whereas those on the bottom reflect upon their predicament and have to find ways to deal with their subordination. They may accept the domination, actively assist others who like themselves are perceived as oppressed, or engage in revolutionary action—but the point is that those who are subordinate are the ones who have to explore the alternatives and devise appropriate strategies. As society responds more and more to the women's movement, we would expect to find a greater variety of female graffiti, reflecting a combination of alternative strategies.[7] Those in a superordinate position, on the other hand, will perpetuate an ideology designed to maintain the status quo. Men express hate in their graffiti and proclaim the inferiority of Jews, blacks, homosexuals, and women. To the extent that subordinate groups are intimidated, accept the imputed inferiority, or acknowledge the flawed character structure attributed to them, they acquiesce in their own domination. In these respects, the underlying message in both male and female graffiti is fundamentally political.

Graffiti reflect the differential positions of men and women in the social structure. Men are dominant; their graffiti reaffirms the macho man who denigrates and controls all out-groups, including women. Women are subordinate; their advisory helpful graffiti tells us they are actively rethinking their relationship to men, to themselves, and to the larger society. Although shorthand phrases are descriptively inadequate, we are now in a position to fill in the fourfold paradigm as follows:

	male	female
surface	competitive-egocentric more derogatory	advisory-interpersonal less derogatory
underlying	reaffirm dominance maintain status quo	rethink subordination explore alternatives

To what extent may these conclusions be generalized? The data for our study and for many other studies of graffiti were gathered on college campuses and may not be representative of the larger society. We can envision a broad scale comparative study analyzing male-female graffiti for different age groups, socioeconomic levels, and regions of the country. In our hypothetical study we see a social matrix of graffiti writings for Protestants, Catholics, Jews, various European ethnic groups, Mexican-Americans, blacks, and native Americans. We would seek out populations of women who have entered the marketplace in direct competition with men and would compare their graffiti with the inscriptions produced by women who have remained in the domestic sphere. We would apply sophisticated statistical techniques that would enable us to maintain the structural regularities in the data, and would balance this with an ethnographic analysis of group relations and stratification in each local situation. Then we would replicate the study in England! To speculate further, we would confront the question that we and all previous students of restroom graffiti have avoided—exactly who are the graffiti writers? If we had an answer to this question it would no longer be necessary to infer the author from the text, a shaky procedure at best. Instead of generalizing about men and women, we could with greater confidence generalize about the men and women who write graffiti. But then what about the readers? All this is in the future of course, for the next study.

Our present study shows, however, that such humble data as toilet graffiti analyzed from a semiotic perspective as texts, structures of meaning, may illuminate basic society processes (Roland Barthes, 1979). We learn about the differences in communication patterns in same-sex encounters and about the silent political discourse conducted by men and by women. The methodology of our study may be innovative compared to previous positivistic research, but our distinction between surface and underlying levels is hardly new. In fact, if we have learned anything from the past century of social science research, from such monumental thinkers as Marx, Freud, and Levi-Strauss, it is that we must not take at face value the mythology, the literal message, produced by, respectively, capitalistic society, neurotics, and primitive tribes. The same applies to men and to women. It is just common sense not to accept a people's manifest mythology about themselves, but to go beyond the words to the underlying meaning. This we have tried to do, and have seen in scribblings in the walls of toilet stalls a serious political discourse.

Notes

1. We thank Nina Baym, Alan Dundes, Claire Farrer, Larry Grossberg, Joan Huber and Armine Kotin for helpful suggestions.

2. Fieldwork was conducted by Jane Paige Kelso for an undergraduate honors program in anthropology at Illinois.

3. Dundes (1966) was the first to use this term.

4. David Grove kindly made these materials available.

5. A statistically significant finding (X^2 = 99.89, p < .01). The sorting decisions were checked by four independent judges.

6. Larry Danielson provided these data.

7. Other examples of women's graffiti that we have seen recently differed from our original sample in that there was a greater emphasis on lesbian themes, the women's movement, and derogation of men. These more recent emphases, however, still conform to our basic interpretation of female graffiti as a political statement made in reference to male domination.

References

Abel, Ernest L. and Barbara E. Buckley, 1977, *The Handwriting on the Wall: Toward a Sociology and Psychology of Graffiti.* Wesport, Connecticut: Greenwood Press.

Alexander, Bob, 1978, "Male and Female Rest Room Graffiti." *Maledicta* 11:42-59.

Aries, Elizabeth, 1976, "Interaction Patterns and Themes of Male, Female, and Mixed Groups." *Small Group Behavior* 7:7-18.

Asher, Linda, 1979, "Women's Wallflowerings." *Psychology Today* 13:12.

Barthes, Roland, 1979, *The Eiffel Tower and Other Mythologies.* New York: Hill and Wang.

Carlson, Rae, 1971, "Sex Differences in Ego Functioning." *Journal of Consulting and Clinical Psychology* 37:267-276.

Dundes, Alan, 1966, "Here I Sit—a Study of American Latrinalia." *Krober Anthropological Society Papers* 34:91-105.

Gadpaille, W. J., 1971, "Graffiti—Its Psychodynamic Significance." *Sexual Behavior* 2:45-51.

Gonos, George, Virginia Mulkern, and Nicholas Poushinsky, 1976, "Anonymous Expression: A Structural View of Graffiti." *Journal of American Folklore* 89:40-48.

Greenberg, Joel, 1979, "Off the Wall at UMass." *Science News* 116:268.

Jenkins, Lee and Cheris Kramer, 1978, "Small Group Process: Learning from Women." *Women's Studies International Quarterly* 1:67-84.

Kalcik, Susan, 1975, ". . . like Ann's Gynecologist or the Time I Was Almost Raped: Personal Narratives in Women's Rape Groups." In Claire R. Farrer, ed., *Women and Folklore.* Austin: University of Texas Press.

Kinsey, Alfred C., Wardell B. Pomeroy, Clyde E. Martin and Paul H. Gebhard, 1953, *Sexual Behavior in the Human Female.* Philadelphia: W. B. Saunders.

Landy, Eugene E. and John M. Steele, 1967, "Graffiti as a Function of Building Utilization." *Perceptual and Motor Skills* 25:711-712.

Lomas, Harvey D., 1973, "Graffiti: Some Observations and Speculations." *The Psychoanalytic Review* 60:71-89.

Longenecker, Gregory J., 1977, "Sequential Parody Graffiti." *Western Folklore* 36:354-364.

Martilla, Luana, 1971, "Write on!—goodbye to female compliance." In W. J. Gadpaille, "Graffiti: Its Psychodynamic Significance." *Sexual Behavior* 2:49.

Mitchell, Carol A., 1977, "The Sexual Perspective in the Appreciation and Interpretation of Jokes." *Western Folklore* 36:303-329.

Peretti, Peter O., Richard Carter, and Betty McClinton, 1977, "Graffiti and Adolescent Personality." *Adolescence* 12:31-42.

Reich, Wendy, Rosalie Buss, Ellen Fein, and Terry Kurtz, 1977, "Notes on Women's Graffiti." *Journal of American Folklore* 90:188-191.

Sechrest, Lee and Luis Flores, 1969, "Homosexuality in the Philippines and the United States: The Handwriting on the Wall." *Journal of Social Psychology* 79:3-12.

Sechrest, Lee and A. Kenneth Olson, 1971, "Graffiti in Four Types of Institutions of Higher Education." *Journal of Sex Research* 7:62-71.

Solomon, Henry and Howard Yager, 1976, "Authoritarianism and Graffiti." *Journal of Social Psychology* 97:149-150.

Stocker, Terrance L., Linda W. Dutcher, Stephen M. Hargrove, and Edwin H. Cook, 1972, "Social Analysis of Graffiti." *Journal of American Folklore* 85:356-366.

Wales, Elizabeth and Barbara Brewer, 1976, "Graffiti in the 1970's." *Journal of Social Psychology* 99:115-23.

My interest in Friendship, and the interest on which it is based, derives from fieldwork that I had done in East Africa. In Uganda, I had studied the social organization of urban-based civil servants who moved (or were transferred) from one city or town to another. Although it might be predicted that such mobility would be disruptive of their social relationships, in fact, the pattern of their movement and the recurrent interaction associated with it supported enduring but intermittently activated friendships. The primary question of that research was the ways in which continuity in work life sustained friendships.

A few years after returning to Africa, I began fieldwork among a different population but related problem by studying the social consequences of unemployment among aerospace and defense engineers in the Boston area. In many respects, these engineers were similar to Ugandan civil servants: they were residentially mobile, but their work provided a sense of continuity which underlay their friendships. Between 1969 and 1972, many of these engineers lost their jobs. This fact provided an opportunity to examine the impact of changes in the expectation of continuity in social life. The problem became: if work was the foundation of their friendships, would unemployment undermine them? In short, doing fieldwork among civil servants in Uganda and among engineers in Boston provided material for a comparative analysis of the role of continuity in social life.

FAIR-WEATHER FRIEND

Label and Context in Middle Class Friendships

DAVID JACOBSON

"Although social anthropologists themselves live lives in which friendship is probably just as important as kinship, and a good deal more problematic to handle, in our professional writings we dwell at length upon kinship and have much less to say about friendship" (Paine, 1969: 505). This paper on friendship in our own society aims toward closing this gap.

Much sociological and anthropological writing about friendship focuses on its properties as an interpersonal relationship. Paine's analysis of friendship, for example, concerns the conduct between friends, and in particular the rules of relevancy that determine "what is permissible or desirable in the relationship." The utility of the concept of rules of relevancy is that it moves the analysis of friendship beyond an account of the attributes of friends and of the rights and duties of friendship to the study of the dynamics of the friend relationship and its contextual variations. This paper also examines friendship contextually, but in a different sense.

Rather than view friendship simply as an interpersonal relationship, either in terms of the attributes of friends or in terms of the behavior between them, the term "friend" is considered as a label that one person attaches to another or to himself with reference to another. My concern with contextual analysis is not with the content or conduct of the relationship, but with the labeling process itself, that is, with the situations in which a person gives and takes away the label of "friend."

The analytical perspective draws on the tradition in social anthropology that emphasizes the situational selection of social identities (cf. Evans-Pritchard, 1940; Leach, 1954; Barth, 1969). In a recent and useful explication of the model Bloch (1971) distinguishes between the moral and tactical meanings of a role-word as it relates to the difference between the "right" and "wrong" conduct associated with a role and the ways in which the role-word is used to transform social relationships and social situations.[1]

Although situational analysis has been used in various anthropological studies, it constitutes a relatively unusual approach in the literature on friendship.[2] Studies of friendship range from those concerned with simply defining the term "friend" or the characteristics of friends to those focusing more on processes such as recruitment into or the formation of friendships. On this continuum, there are five major types of analysis. In the most simple sort, a single definition of the term "friend" is assumed and the primary effort is to analyze the attributes of friends within a singular context. Little attention is paid to types of friends, to contexts of interaction, or to changes in relationships. The best examples of this type are sociometric studies, in which individuals encapsulated within a population—typically a room of school children, a high school's students, or the residents of a college dormitory—are asked to name their friends within that unit, and then the socio-demographic characteristics of these choices are analyzed with reference to their similarities and differences. Common attributes are then interpreted as the basis for, or the definition of, friendship (see, for example, Thorpe, 1955, and similar studies cited by Albert and Brigante, 1962).

A related but somewhat more developed type of study takes the role "friend," still an undefined and undifferentiated category, and contrasts it with other social identities (kin and neighbors are the most common) in order to analyze the structure and functions of friendship (see Litwak and Szelenyi, 1969). This method of comparative analysis goes byond the sociometric studies in its attempt to make explicit the rights and duties of friendship. However the category of friend remains undifferentiated, and the dynamics of the relationship, including the movement of personnel between those roles, remains unexamined. Consequently, the findings of this type of study are often ambiguous. Although the different social identities in question are distinguished analytically, little or no attention is paid to the fact that empirically the differentiation is not easily discernible, and that the same person may occupy all of them, being kinsman, neighbor, and friend simultaneously. Behavior that is attributed to kinship may be equally attributable to friendship or to the relationship between neighbors.

A third type of study is still largely definitional, but provides a more differentiated and more realistic account of friendship. Naegele (1958), for example, describes "acquaintances," "friends," and "close friends" and notes the development of a relationship as it moves from a casual personal contact to one more intimate. The movement is described as unidirectional. No attention is given to reverses in a relationship or to its termination, whatever stage of its development; process is still not a focal concern.

A fourth approach focuses more on interactional processes and deals with the dynamics of friendship (see Suttles, 1970). Suttles suggests that a friend is someone who is positively evaluated as a person qua person; therefore, true friendship requires revelation of one's true self, not the self (or selves) governed by norms conventional to social situations. This line of thought leads Suttles to argue that the "logic of friendship is a simple transformation of the rules of public propriety into their opposite" (1970: 116). Although Suttles analyzes this logic, his study is still about the (normative) characteristics of the relationship—how individuals who are friends are supposed to act towards one another—and, in this sense, resembles Paine's examination of the "rules of relevancy," which are said to regulate behavior between friends.[3] Although Suttles recognizes the problems his analysis does not deal with exceptions to these rules or with the ways in which friendships begin or end.

The fifth type of study complements the others by analyzing the dissolution of friendships in order to illuminate the processes underlying their formation and maintenance. Liebow's description of the changing friendships of "streetcorner men" (1967) is one of the best of its kind. Liebow depicts their friendships in term of a network radiating out from an Ego. In its inner part, closest to the focal individual (Ego), are "good" and "best" friends and on its outer edges are "acquaintances" and "former friends" (1967: 162-163). The category of "former friends," in particular, is important in its implication of oscillation, suggesting not only the beginnings of relationships but their endings as well. Liebow analyzes the transition from acquaintance to friend to best friend, emphasizing the motivation for the transformation, which, he suggests, is primarily instrumental. Friends exchange goods and services, necessary for survival among those who face chronic poverty. Reciprocity is promised between friends, but the reality of limited resources restrains individuals from meeting expectations, leading to the breakdown of relationships and to a corresponding reevaluation of people as "fair-weather friends." Leibow thus relates changes in the identification of friends, of those who are included and excluded under that label, to changing socioeconomic circumstances. He analyzes this labeling process among the urban poor, but it also occurs in middle-class friendships, as is evident among unemployed professional workers.

My data come largely from a study of unemployed engineers.[4] The saliency of the label "friend" in this population derives from the fact that engineers find jobs primarily through friends. In fact, whatever other rights and duties obtain between friends, it is a paramount expectation among engineers that a friend will help another who is in search of employment. Furthermore, a person who proves to be a contact in getting a job is often described as a friend, regardless of whether or not that person acts as such in other respects. Alternatively, an individual who does not offer assistance in finding a job may be described as "no friend," or, at best, as a "fair-weather friend."

The analysis, then, focuses on the term "friend" as a label, and on the contexts in which it is applied and withdrawn. The conditions under which engineers include and exclude others as members of their social world is also of particular concern.

Route 128, ringing Boston, Massachusetts has been described as the eastern center of the electronics industry in the United States. Predominant in this area are major corporations and their satellite companies involved in federally funded aerospace and defense research. Because of government funding cutbacks, between 1969 and 1972 large numbers of engineers and scientists were laid off. My interest here is in how these unemployed professional workers used their contacts with friends in the search for another job.

Before describing the process, some features of employment in these companies must be noted. To begin with, such companies typically work on projects supported by various agencies of the federal government. When a contract for a project is awarded, and sometimes in anticipation of one, a company hires the necessary scientific and technological personnel. When it is completed, the employment of those engineers and scientists is also terminated. Few of these employees are maintained on in-house funds so that tenured or permanent positions are unusual. Therefore, engineers and scientists typically find themselves having to periodically seek work or moving between jobs, even in times of continuing governmental support and relatively full employment. Of course, at those times, employment in one company might be practically continuous, since the company may be working on several projects, simultaneously or sequentially. Even then, though, the demand for labor is not uniform, varying with phases in a project from its inception to its completion; and engineers and scientists are often moved, or have the opportunity to move, between projects, within and between companies. With this characteristic mobility between jobs, engineers and scientists participate in "occupational contact networks" (Katz, 1958), through which information about jobs is communicated between colleagues. It is in these networks that friends are important.

The concept "friend," for the engineers, is a general term and implies various expectations in the relationship between those involved. Unmodified, it may connote more particular role-words, which can be verbally differentiated: for example, "close" friend, "old" friend, or "acquaintance." The term "friend," then, unspecified, refers to a range of individuals and relationships. Specific rights and duties are distributed differently among particular kinds of friends, by which they are contrasted with one another and thereby distinguished. For example, a close friend may be permitted to pay an unannounced visit to one's home—that is, to simply and informally drop in, while such behavior would be unexpected and perhaps discouraged from others. Whatever the differences between categories, however, all friends are expected to help one another in the process of getting a job, although it is recognized that different sorts of friends will go to greater or lesser lengths in providing such assistance.

The data on actual job contacts support the normative rule that friends help one another in getting a job. Asked about past job contacts (i.e., about leads to getting a job before the period of government cutbacks and unemployment), 67 percent of the engineers studied said that they got their jobs through friends. This figure is consistent with that found by other researchers. Shapero, Howell, and Tombaugh published a study describing the Los Angeles and Boston centers of the defense research and development industry. They reported that 51 percent of the engineers and scientists they interviewed found their jobs through "personal acquaintances" (1965: 50). Although "personal acquaintance" is not explicitly defined, the authors use it interchangeably with the word "friend" (1965: 50). Similar results were uncovered by Granovetter whose study of technical, professional, and managerial workers indicated that 55 percent got their jobs through "personal contacts" (1974: 19). In this instance, it is clear that personal contacts are friends (1974: 16, 41, 165). Although there are some differences in the population composition and the way in which respondents describe job contacts, the overall pattern is clear: when the job market is good for professional workers, friends are a primary source of job contacts.

When the market is bad, however, friends do not play an equally important role in getting a job. The data I have on the ways in which unemployed engineers and scientists find work support this claim. By the beginning of 1973, most (89 percent) of those I had interviewed earlier had been rehired. Of these, 31 percent had found jobs through friends, the others getting jobs through impersonal formal channels, including ads, agencies, professional associations, and direct application. This figure is close to that found in an earlier study by Mooney (1965) of job information channels among unemployed engineers and scientists. He reported that of those reemployed, 27 percent got jobs through a "friend or relative" (1965: 152).

Here, then, is the problem. When jobs are easily available and engineers and scientists are in demand, friends are important job contacts, as is evident by the fact that from one-half to two-thirds of these professional workers get their jobs through friends. When jobs are scarce, however, the percentage of jobs found through friends drops to between one-third and one-fourth.

There are least two alternative interpretations to account for this fluctuation. The first is that assuming the category of friends includes colleagues who have more or less the same information about jobs, then friends will not have different or additional information about job possibilities and therefore will not be in a position to help. But job contacts are still made through friends, even though the number of such contacts is reduced. Thus, another hypothesis is required to account for the differential use of friends in loose and tight markets.

The second explanation is that friends who are colleagues will be in competition with one another for scarce resources, including information about prospective employment opportunities. As a result they withhold or selectively distribute information, in which case there will be some manipulation or reclassification as to who counts as a friend. This interpretation accords with the idea that the term "friend" is polysemic and has a tactical meaning reflecting changing social situations. In this sense the word "friend," meaning in particular "close" friend, describes those who are situationally labeled as such and from whom the label is withdrawn as circumstances dictate, thereby avoiding the obligations of the relationship. These are fair-weather friends. This interpretation is supported by the following facts.

The distinction between close friend and fair-weather friend as different meanings of the word "friend" used in its unmodified form, is apparent in some of the studies already mentioned. Granovetter, for example, notes that the word "friend," as a general term used in describing job contacts, in fact refers to two kinds of friends: "social friends" and "work contacts" (1974: 41-42). This classification corresponds to the differentiation between close friend and the sort of friend whose relationship might be situationally emphasized or deemphasized. Granovetter further reports that of those getting a job through a friend, 31.4 percent involved "social" or "close" friends and 68.7 percent involved "work contacts." What is particularly interesting about the two meanings of "friend" identified by Granovetter is that if "work-contact" friends are indeed fair-weather friends, then when the demand for engineers is depressed, one would expect that such friends would drop out of the friend category. Those who remained as job contacts would be those otherwise identifiable as "close" friends. This is consistent with the difference noted before between the larger number of friends reported as job contacts under favorable circumstances and the smaller number associated with a tight market.

A similar pattern of the meaning of "friend" emerges from Laumann's study of friendship networks. Laumann found, somewhat to his surprise, that "work-based" friendships differ from "close" friendships in that while close friendships are enduring, work-based friendships are easily formed and easily broken (1973: 93-96). Although Laumann does not analyze the conditions under which work-based friendships are broken, we might predict, in light of the fair-weather friend hypothesis, that this would happen when the job market was tight or when the work situation otherwise changed.

Furthermore, the distinction between the meanings of "friend" helps to clarify certain ambiguities in recent research in Boston by Powell and Driscoll (1973) among unemployed professionals. Powell and Driscoll interviewed unemployed middle-class professionals, mostly engineers, at an employment center in Massachusetts. I worked with the same category of people, in the same place, and approximately at the same time. Our two samples have similar sociodemographic characteristics, yet our findings of the social consequences of unemployment for these men differ as a result of the different meanings associated with "friend." Powell and Driscoll describe a progressive deterioration of friendship among these men from the onset of unemployment. At first there is no change in relations between friends; then relationships begin to break down, although here there is some ambiguity, because some friends are said to offer help while others engage in avoidance behavior; finally, relationships with others are limited to a few very close friends. The men I interviewed described the effects of unemployment on their friendships quite differently. For example, none of the men interviewed said that there had been a negative change in his friendships; 96 percent said that there had been no change at all. Although accounts from individuals in the two samples of unemployed men appear to be inconsistent, even contradictory, I think their experiences, in fact, may be quite similar and that the differences between them derive, in part, from differences in the interpretations they placed on these experiences.

The major difference is associated with the meaning attributed to the term "friend." Powell and Driscoll assume that the term has a single and fixed referent. By contrast, for the men I interviewed, the concept of friendship is polysemic. "Friend," for them, involves a relatively large class or set of people, including "old" friends, "close" friends, and those who, by further specification of situation or context, would otherwise be identified as "acquaintance" or "business associate." Thus, my informants, like those of Powell and Driscoll, report that one correlation of unemployment is a restriction in the circle of friends, a limitation of interaction to those who can be described as "close" friends. These men, however, did not describe this process as a breakdown in friendships, but rather as one that involves a more rigorous, a more selective (situationally specific) definition or redefinition of who is a friend. In other words, they say that they have, and have had, a small set of friends, with whom there has been no change in relationship since becoming unemployed. There are also others, now described as "just a friend," an acquaintance, or a business associate, with whom the relationship has changed. Thus, unemployment, representing a change of circumstances or conditions, induces a change in the labeling process, a change in those identified as friend, but not in the structure of rights and duties (i.e., in the relationships between friends). This change in labeling, the contraction of the set of people described as friends, explains, I think, the ambiguity in the account of Powell and Driscoll: that some friends are said to offer help to the unemployed, but that other friends are said to avoid them. Those who offer help are counted as close friends and no change is reported in those relationships. Those who turn away—who refuse to help and who thereby fail to recognize or meet what is understood to be a characteristic and an obligation of friendship—are no longer friends.

This analysis is meant to contribute to an understanding of friendship in our society. I suggest that anthropological inquiry, including semantic and situational analyses, will supplement the knowledge generated by those working within other disciplines precisely because it does not assume the meaning of a term. Rather anthropology takes as a primary task the analysis of its meanings as these vary across different social contexts.

Notes

This paper was read in draft form in the symposium "North of the Border: Anthropological Inquiries into American Culture and Society" at the 73rd Annual Meeting of the American Anthropological Association, November 1974 (Mexico City).

1. Similar to Bloch's concept of "tactical meaning" is the idea of a "metaphoric use" of a term, "based on connotative meaning . . . to imply solidarity of a sort, and a mode of conduct between the parties concerned, which is similar in some limited respect to that appropiate to [those] who are designated by [the] terms" (Scheffler and Lounsbury, 1971: 9).

2. The literature on friendship is diverse; the most useful introductions to it are Coelho (1959) and Paine (1970).

3. The analyses of Paine and Suttles differ from the sociometric studies in their emphasis on the characteristics of social relationships rather than those of the participants in them.

4. Research in 1971-1972 was supported by a grant (MH-20222-01) from the National Institute of Mental Health, to which I express my appreciation.

References

Albert, Robert S. and T. R. Brigante, 1962, "The Psychology of Friendship Relations: Social Factors." *The Journal of Social Psychology* 56:33-47.

Barth, Fredrik, 1969, *Ethnic Groups and Boundaries.* Boston: Little, Brown.

Bloch, Maurice, 1971, "The Moral and Tactical Meaning of Kinship Terms." *Man* (N.S.) 6, no. 1:79-87.

Coelho, George V., 1959, "A Guide to Literature on Friendship: A Selectively Annotated Bibliography." *Pscyhological Newsletter* 10:365-394.

Evans-Pritchard, E.E., 1940, *The Nuer.* London: Oxford University Press.

Granovetter, Mark S., 1974, *Getting a Job.* Cambridge, Mass.: Harvard University Press.

Katz, Fred, 1958, "Occupational Contact Networks." *Social Forces* 37: 52-58.

Thorpe, J. G., 1955, "A Study of Some Factors in Friendship Formation." *Sociometry* 18, no. 3: 207-214.

Laumann, Edward O., 1973, *Bonds of Pluralism: The Form and Substance of Urban Social Networks.* New York: Wiley.

Leach, E. R., 1954, *Political Systems of Highland Burma.* London: Bell.

Liebow, Elliot, 1967, *Tally's Corner.* Boston: Little, Brown.

Litwak, E. and I. Szelenyi, 1969, "Primary Group Structures and Their Functions: Kin, Neighbors, and Friends." *American Sociological Review,* 34, no. 4:465-481.

Mooney, Joseph D., 1965, "Displaced Engineers and Scientists; An Analysis of the Labor Market Adjustment of Professional Personnel." Unpublished Ph.D. dissertation. Cambridge: Massachusetts Institute of Technology.

Naegele, Kaspar D., 1958, "Friendship and Acquaintances: An Exploration of Some Social Distinctions." *Harvard Educational Review* 28, no. 3:232-

252.

Paine, Robert, 1969, "In Search of Friendship: An Exploratory Analysis in 'Middle-Class' Culture." *Man* (N.S.), 4, no. 4:505-524.

—"Anthropological Approaches to Friendship." *Humanitas* 6, no. 2:

Powell, Douglas H. and Paul F. Driscoll, 1973, "Middle Class Professionals Face Unemployment." *Society*, 10, no. 2:18-26.

Scheffler, Harold W. and Floyd G. Lounsbury, 1971, *A Study in Structural Semantics.* Englewood Cliffs, N.J.: Prentice Hall.

Shapero, Albert, Richard P. Howell, and James R. Tombaugh, 1965, *The Structure and Dynamics of the Defense R and D Industry.* Menlo Park, Calif.: Stanford Research Institute.

Suttles, Gerald, 1970, "Friendship as a Social Institution." In George McCall et al., *Social Relationships.* Pp. 95-135. Chicago: Aldine.